Mediterranean Diet

Cookbook

for Beginners

Delicious Recipes, Practical Tips, and a Comprehensive 28-Day Meal Plan for a Healthier Lifestyle

BY

Elena Santorini

Scan the QR code below to join our list for announcements of other cookbooks we publish

Page left blank

Page left blank

Contents

Introduction

The Mediterranean Diet is a way of eating that has been cherished for centuries by people living in countries bordering the Mediterranean Sea. This diet is not just about your food; it's a lifestyle that emphasizes balance, variety, and enjoying meals with family and friends.

This book, Mediterranean Diet Cookbook for Beginners, provides a simple, authentic guide to embracing the Mediterranean Diet. Whether you want to improve your health, manage your weight, or enjoy delicious and wholesome meals, this book will be your companion on this journey.

You will learn about the origins and science behind the Mediterranean Diet, understand its numerous health benefits, and discover how to incorporate its principles into your daily life. This book is intended to be accessible and easy to follow, so you may reap the benefits of the Mediterranean Diet without feeling overwhelmed. Along the way, you'll find various recipes that reflect this diet's authentic flavors and health benefits, making it simple to prepare delicious and nutritious meals for every occasion.

CHAPTER 1

Welcome to the Mediterranean Diet

Brief History and Origins

The Mediterranean Diet originates from the traditional eating practices of Greece, Italy, and Spain. This diet emerged from the region's natural bounty, rich in fruits, vegetables, grains, nuts, and olive oil, with fish and seafood from the surrounding seas. Historically, people relied on locally available foods and cultural practices emphasizing plant-based meals and fish. These dietary habits were influenced by the region's warm climate, fertile soil, and cultural and religious traditions that promoted the consumption of wholesome, minimally processed foods.

In the mid-20th century, American scientist Ancel Keys conducted the Seven Countries Study, discovering that populations in the Mediterranean had lower rates of heart disease and longer lifespans. Keys attributed their health benefits to a diet high in plant-based foods, good fats, and lean protein. Today, the Mediterranean Diet is celebrated globally for its multiple health benefits, including a lower risks of heart disease, diabetes, and certain cancers. It is widely recommended by nutritionists and healthcare professionals for its emphasis on fresh, whole foods and balanced meals, making it both delicious and beneficial for long-term health.

The Science Behind the Diet

The Mediterranean Diet is supported by extensive scientific research highlighting its numerous health benefits. This diet concentrates the consumption of whole, minimally processed foods rich in nutrients and antioxidants. The primary components include fruits, vegetables, whole grains, legumes, nuts, olive oil, and moderate fish and poultry. A key finding is that the Mediterranean Diet is high in monounsaturated fats, primarily from olive oil, which can help reduce harmful cholesterol levels and improve heart health. Monounsaturated fats lower low-density lipoprotein (LDL) cholesterol without affecting high-density lipoprotein (HDL) cholesterol, which benefits cardiovascular health. Olive oil also contains polyphenols with anti-inflammatory and antioxidant properties, further improving heart health.

The diet also contains omega-3 fatty acids from fish including salmon, mackerel, and sardines. Omega-3 fatty acids decrease inflammation, lower blood pressure, reduce triglyceride levels, and minimize the chances of heart disease. These substances are linked to improved cognitive function and a decreased risk of neurodegenerative diseases. They are crucial for maintaining the health of the brain. Another critical aspect of the Mediterranean Diet is its high fiber content, derived from fruits, vegetables, whole grains, and legumes. Dietary fiber is vital for maintaining digestive health, promoting regular bowel movements, and preventing constipation. Additionally, fiber lowers the risk of type 2 diabetes by delaying the bloodstream's absorption of sugar. This helps to normalize blood sugar levels.

Antioxidants like flavonoids, carotenoids, and vitamins C and E are found in diets rich in plants and play an important role in protecting cells from the damaging impacts of free radicals. Free radicals are unstable compounds that have the potential to create oxidative stress, which increases the chances of chronic illnesses like diabetes, cancer, and cardiovascular disease, as well as prolonged inflammation. The high intake of antioxidant-rich foods in the Mediterranean Diet helps neutralize free radicals, reducing oxidative stress and inflammation. In addition to its macronutrient composition, the Mediterranean Diet includes a variety of micronutrients that contribute to overall health.

Nuts and seeds provide essential minerals such as magnesium, zinc, and selenium, which improve immune function, bone health, and metabolic processes. Overall, the Mediterranean Diet's emphasis on balanced, nutrient-rich foods contributes to its effectiveness in promoting long-term health and preventing various diseases. This scientific backing makes it a highly recommended dietary pattern by health professionals worldwide.

Health Benefits

The Mediterranean Diet is celebrated for its extensive health benefits, making it a top recommendation by healthcare professionals. One of its primary advantages is its positive impact on heart health. The diet's emphasis on healthy fats from olive oil and a high intake of fruits, vegetables, whole grains, and fish helps reduce the risk of cardiovascular diseases. Research shows that individuals following this diet have improved cholesterol levels and lower blood pressure, contributing to better overall heart health. In addition to cardiovascular benefits, the Mediterranean Diet is effective in managing and preventing type 2 diabetes. Whole grains, vegetables, fruits and legumes contain a significant amount of fiber content, which helps maintain blood sugar and improve insulin sensitivity. The diet's anti-inflammatory properties, derived from omega-3 fatty acids, antioxidants, and polyphenols, also play a vital role in lessening the chance of chronic diseases, including diabetes and certain cancers.

The Mediterranean diet helps people control their weight and promotes overall longevity. Its focus on nutrient-dense, whole foods aids in maintaining a healthy weight. The diet also encourages mindful eating practices and the enjoyment of meals with family and friends, which benefits mental health and reduces the risk of depression and anxiety. Additionally, the diet's rich content of antioxidants and healthy fats benefits brain health, lowering the risk of neurodegenerative diseases like Alzheimer's and Parkinson's. Overall, the Mediterranean Diet promotes physical and mental well-being, offering a holistic approach to health.

Key Health Benefits

- **Heart Health:** Reduces LDL (bad) cholesterol, improves HDL (good) cholesterol, and lowers blood pressure.

- **Diabetes Management:** Stabilizes blood sugar levels and enhances insulin sensitivity.

- **Anti-inflammatory Effects:** Lowers the risk of chronic diseases such as certain cancers.

- **Weight Management:** Provides balanced, nutrient-rich meals that help maintain a healthy weight.

- **Mental Health:** Encourages mindful eating and social interactions, reducing the risk of depression and anxiety.

- **Brain Health:** Lowers the risk of neurodegenerative diseases like Alzheimer's and Parkinson's.

Understanding the Mediterranean Diet

The traditional eating practices of countries like Greece, Italy, and Spain are the foundation of the Mediterranean diet, which is a way of life. It emphasizes fresh, whole foods and minimally processed ingredients. The diet prioritizes plant-based foods like fruits, vegetables, whole grains, legumes, and nuts. These foods are filled with fiber, antioxidants, and other nutrients that help maintain good health and prevent disease. Healthy fats, particularly from olive oil, are a cornerstone of the Mediterranean Diet. Monounsaturated fats found in olive oil, which is used in cooking and as a dressing, are good for the heart. Nuts, seeds, and avocados are other foods that provide good fats. Seafood and fish have a lot of omega-3 fatty acids that promote heart and brain health, are the main sources of protein. In moderation, poultry, eggs, and dairy products such as yogurt and cheese are included as extra sources of protein and calcium. Red meat is limited in the Mediterranean Diet, typically eaten only a few times a month. Instead, meals are often centered around fish, legumes, and plant-based proteins. Sweets and sugary foods are also kept to a minimum and reserved for special occasions. This lowers the chance of developing chronic diseases and promotes general health by helping to maintain a balanced diet.

A unique aspect of the Mediterranean Diet is its focus on social eating. Sharing meals with family and friends encourages mindful eating and a relaxed approach to food, enhancing digestion and overall satisfaction. Additionally, regular physical activity, such as walking and gardening, is integral to the Mediterranean lifestyle. Both physical and mental well-being are enhanced by leading an active lifestyle and eating a balanced diet.

The Mediterranean Diet offers a sustainable and enjoyable way to maintain a healthy lifestyle. Focusing on fresh, whole foods and balanced meals provides numerous health benefits and promotes long-term well-being.

Principles of the Mediterranean Diet

The Mediterranean Diet is built on several core principles that emphasize balance, variety, and enjoyment of food. Understanding these principles can help you incorporate this healthy eating pattern into your daily life.

Emphasis on Plant-Based Foods: Most of the Mediterranean Diet consists of plant-based foods, including fruits, vegetables, whole grains, legumes, and nuts. These foods enhance overall health and well-being because they are important source of fiber, vitamins, and minerals. To guarantee that your meal is full of a variety of nutrients, try loading it up with vibrant fruits and veggies.

Healthy Fats: Healthy fats, particularly from olive oil, are a staple in the Mediterranean Diet. Olive oil is used in cooking, as a dressing, and even as a dip for bread. It provides monounsaturated fats that help reduce harmful cholesterol levels and promote heart health. Avocados, nuts, and seeds are additional sources of healthy fats. Incorporating these fats into your meals can improve your lipid profile and provide essential fatty acids.

Moderate Protein Intake: The major provider of protein in the Mediterranean diet is seafood, especially fish, which is high in fatty acids known as omega-3. These fats boost cardiovascular health and have anti-inflammatory qualities. Eating fish is recommended to occur no less than twice a week. In moderation, poultry, eggs, and dairy products like cheese and yogurt are added as well to provide extra protein and calcium. Red meat is limited and typically eaten only a few times a month.

Limited Red Meat and Sweets: The Mediterranean Diet sparingly consumes red meat, emphasizing lean proteins like fish and plant-based options. Sweets and sugary foods are also restricted and reserved for special occasions or occasional treats. This lowers consumption of added sugars and saturated fats while promoting a balanced diet.

Whole Grains: Whole grains are a fundamental component of the Mediterranean Diet. Whole wheat bread, brown rice, barley, and quinoa are preferred over refined grains. More fiber, vitamins, and minerals found in whole grains improve healthy digestion and help to keep blood sugar levels consistent.

Fresh and Seasonal Foods: The Mediterranean Diet encourages the consumption of fresh, seasonal foods. This ensures better taste and nutritional value and promotes local farming and sustainability. Eating a variety of seasonal produce can enhance your diet's nutritional diversity and provide a richer culinary experience.

Mindful and Social Eating: The Mediterranean diet's unique principle of mindful and social eating focuses on slow, shared meals. This practice encourages mindfulness, better digestion, and greater satisfaction with food. Eating in a relaxed and social environment helps build healthy eating habits and fosters a positive relationship with food.

Regular Physical Activity: Besides dietary habits, regular physical activity is integral to the Mediterranean lifestyle. Activities such as walking, gardening, and moderate exercise are encouraged daily. Exercise improves cardiovascular health, helps people maintain a healthy weight, and enhances general well-being, all of which are benefits of adding physical exercise to diet.

What to Eat and How Often

Understanding what to eat and how often is crucial to successfully adopting the Mediterranean Diet. This section guides the types of foods to include in your diet and their recommended consumption frequency.

Daily Foods

- **Fruits and Vegetables:** Make it a daily goal to incorporate various kinds of fruits and veggies into your meals. These should form the basis of your diet, providing essential vitamins, minerals, and fiber. Strive for at least five servings of vegetables and 2-4 servings of fruit daily.

- **Whole Grains:** Include whole grains in your regular meals, such as quinoa, barley, brown rice, oats, and whole wheat bread. B vitamins, fiber, and other vital nutrients abound in these grains.

- **Healthy Fats:** Your main fat source for cooking and dressings should be olive oil. Seeds and nuts can be added to meals or eaten as snacks. Another great food that is high in healthy fats is avocados.

- **Legumes:** Chickpeas, lentils, and beans should be consumed daily, or at least several times per week. They are great sources of protein, fiber, and other nutrients.

- **Dairy:** Consume moderate amounts of dairy products, such as yogurt and cheese. These provide calcium and protein but should be chosen in their natural, unsweetened forms whenever possible.

Weekly Foods

- **Fish and Seafood:** Aim to eat fish and seafood at least twice weekly. These foods are rich in fatty acids known as omega-3, which are beneficial for heart and brain health. Examples include salmon, mackerel, sardines, and shellfish.

- **Poultry and Eggs:** Include moderate poultry and eggs in your weekly diet. These provide high-quality protein and essential nutrients without red meat's higher saturated fat content.

Occasional Foods

- **Red Meat:** Red meat should be consumed sparingly, typically no more than a few times a month. When you do consume red meat, go for smaller portions and lean cuts.

- **Sweets and Desserts:** Limit sweets and desserts to special occasions. These should not be a regular part of your diet due to their high sugar and calorie content. Choose for fresh fruit, small amounts of nuts, and dark chocolate if you desire a treat.

Beverages

- **Water:** To stay hydrated, drink lots of water throughout the day. Water is the preferred beverage in the Mediterranean Diet.

- **Wine:** Moderate wine consumption, particularly red wine, is often included in the Mediterranean Diet. This usually means up to one glass per day for women and up to two glasses per day for men, typically enjoyed with meals. If you do not drink alcohol, there is no need to start.

Following these guidelines on what to eat and how often, you can effectively embrace the Mediterranean Diet and enjoy its numerous health benefits. This balanced approach to eating emphasizes variety, nutrient-rich foods, and mindful consumption, all of which contribute to a healthier lifestyle.

Stocking Your Pantry

A well-stocked pantry is essential for adopting and maintaining the Mediterranean Diet. Having the right ingredients on hand makes it easier to prepare healthy, delicious meals. Here's a guide to the essential items in your pantry, fridge, and freezer to foster your Mediterranean lifestyle.

Pantry Staples

- **Olive Oil:** Extra virgin olive oil is a cornerstone of the Mediterranean Diet. Use it for cooking, dressing, and drizzling over dishes.

- **Whole Grains:** Stock up on grains like brown rice, quinoa, barley, bulgur, farro, and whole wheat pasta. These provide a nutritious base for many meals.

- **Legumes:** Keep various dried or canned beans and legumes, such as chickpeas, lentils, black beans, and cannellini beans. They are versatile and can be used in soups, salads, and main dishes.

- **Nuts and Seeds:** Almonds, walnuts, sunflower seeds, and chia seeds are excellent for snacking and adding to dishes. For the most health benefits, go for unsalted types.

- **Herbs and Spices:** Spices and dried herbs are essential for adding flavor without extra calories. Common Mediterranean spices include oregano, basil, thyme, rosemary, cumin, and paprika.

- **Canned Tomatoes and Tomato Paste:** These are perfect for making sauces, soups, and stews. Choose varieties with no additional salt whenever you can.

- **Whole Grain Flours:** Keep whole wheat flour and other whole grain flour on hand for baking and cooking.

- **Vinegar:** Balsamic, apple cider vinegar and red wine are great for dressings and marinades.

- **Olives and Capers:** These add flavor to many Mediterranean dishes. Keep a variety of olives and capers in your pantry.

Fridge Essentials

- **Fresh Vegetables:** Stock up on various fresh, seasonal vegetables like tomatoes, cucumbers, bell peppers, leafy greens, zucchini, and eggplant. These are the foundation of many Mediterranean dishes.

- **Fruits:** Keep fresh fruits like apples, oranges, berries, and grapes for snacks and desserts.

- **Dairy:** Yogurt, especially Greek yogurt, and cheeses such as feta, halloumi, and mozzarella are vital components. Choose low-fat or full-fat versions based on your dietary needs.

- **Fish and Seafood:** Fresh fish and seafood should be a regular part of your diet. Look for sustainable options and aim to include them in your meals several times a week.

- **Eggs:** Eggs are a versatile protein source. Keep them on hand for breakfast, lunch, and dinner options.

- **Herbs:** Fresh herbs like parsley, cilantro, basil, and mint add freshness and flavor to your dishes. To increase the shelf life of them, store them correctly.

Freezer Items

- **Frozen Vegetables:** Keep various frozen vegetables on hand for quick and easy meal preparation. They are just as nutritious as fresh and convenient for busy days.

- **Fish and Seafood:** Stock up on frozen fish and seafood to ensure you always have a healthy protein option.

- **Bread:** Whole-grain bread can be frozen and used as needed. This prevents waste and ensures you always have a healthy bread option.

- **Berries and Fruits:** Frozen berries and fruits are excellent for smoothies, baking, and desserts.

By stocking your pantry with these Mediterranean essentials, you'll be well-equipped to prepare nutritious and flavorful meals. It is simpler to follow the Mediterranean diet and reap its health benefits when you have these staples.

CHAPTER 3

Kitchen Tips and Tricks

Essential Kitchen Tools for Mediterranean Cooking

Having the right tools in your kitchen can make cooking Mediterranean dishes more accessible and enjoyable. Here are some essential kitchen tools that will help you prepare delicious **Mediterranean meals:**

- **Olive Oil Dispenser:** Since olive oil is a mainstay of the Mediterranean diet, an olive oil dispenser is a must. A suitable dispenser allows for easy pouring and controlled usage, ensuring you use just the right amount for cooking and dressing salads.

- **Mortar and Pestle:** A mortar and pestle is perfect for grinding fresh herbs and spices, making pesto, and creating other traditional Mediterranean sauces and pastes. This tool helps release the ingredients' natural oils and flavors, enhancing the taste of your dishes.

- **Cast Iron Skillet:** For baking bread, sautéing veggies, and scorching meats, a cast iron pan works great. It is a useful tool for many Mediterranean recipes because of its capacity to hold and transmit heat evenly.

- **Grater or Microplane:** A grater or microplane grates hard cheeses like Parmesan, zesting citrus fruits, and mincing garlic. Mediterranean cuisine frequently uses these ingredients to infuse dishes with flavor and freshness.

- **Salad Spinner:** A salad spinner is handy for washing and drying greens and herbs. Clean, dry greens are essential for making fresh salads and garnishes, a staple in Mediterranean cuisine.

- **Mandoline Slicer:** You can swiftly and evenly slice fruits and vegetables using a mandoline slicer. This tool is perfect for preparing dishes like ratatouille, gratins, and salads where thin, even slices are essential.

- **Food Processor:** A food processor is invaluable for making dips, spreads, and dough. It's beneficial for preparing hummus, baba ganoush, and other Mediterranean dips.

- **Sharp Knives:** Investing in high-quality sharp knives is crucial for efficient and safe cooking. A chef's knife, serrated knife and paring knife are necessary for a variety of jobs, such as slicing bread and chopping vegetables.

- **Cutting Board:** A good cutting board offers a stable, long-lasting surface for chopping and mixing items. Choose a board that is large enough to handle big tasks and easy to clean.

- **Dutch Oven:** A Dutch oven makes soups, stews, and braised dishes. Its heavy construction and tight-fitting lid allow for even cooking and flavor development, making it perfect for Mediterranean one-pot meals.

- **Baking Sheets and Parchment Paper:** Baking sheets and parchment paper are essential for roasting vegetables, baking fish, and making flatbreads. They ensure even cooking and easy cleanup.

- **Measuring Cups and Spoons:** Accurate measurements are essential for following recipes, especially when baking. It's easier to make sure you add the right amount of each ingredient when you have a set of measuring spoons and cups.

Having these basic kitchen items can let you cook a variety of tasty and healthful Mediterranean cuisine. These tools make cooking more efficient and enhance the overall cooking experience, helping you enjoy the process as much as the results.

Mediterranean Cooking Techniques

Mastering key cooking techniques can significantly enhance your ability to prepare delicious and authentic Mediterranean dishes. **These are some key Mediterranean cooking methods that will enhance your culinary abilities and wow your guests:**

- **Grilling:** Grilling is a cornerstone of Mediterranean cuisine, adding a unique smoky flavor to meats, seafood, and vegetables. Whether you use an outdoor or indoor grill pan, this technique is perfect for preparing dishes like kebabs, grilled fish, and vegetables. Brush ingredients with olive oil and season herbs and spices before grilling to enhance the flavors.

- **Sautéing:** Sautéing is a quick and efficient way to cook vegetables, fish, and meats while preserving their natural flavors and nutrients. Use a small amount of olive oil in a hot pan and cook ingredients over medium-high heat, stirring frequently. This technique is ideal for making dishes like sautéed spinach, garlic shrimp, and vegetable medleys.

- **Roasting:** Roasting concentrates the natural sweetness and flavors of vegetables, meats, and fish. Set the temperature of your oven to a high one, toss ingredients with olive oil, salt, and herbs, and spread them evenly on a baking sheet. Roasting is perfect for preparing dishes like roasted root vegetables, baked fish, and Mediterranean-style chicken.

- **Slow Cooking:** Slow cooking is excellent for developing rich, deep flavors in stews, soups, and braised dishes. Place the ingredients in a slow cooker or Dutch oven and simmer over low heat for several hours. This technique is ideal for making hearty dishes like lamb stew, vegetable tagine, and bean soups.

- **Blanching:** Blanching involves briefly boiling vegetables and then plunging them into ice water to stop cooking. This technique helps preserve the color, texture, and nutrients of vegetables. Blanching helps prepare salads, vegetable platters, and dishes that require a quick cooking, like green beans with almonds.

- **Poaching:** Poaching is a gentle cooking method that simmers ingredients in liquid at a low temperature. This technique is often used for cooking delicate foods like fish and eggs. Poaching helps retain moisture and flavor, making it ideal for dishes like poached salmon with dill or eggs in tomato sauce (shakshuka).

- **Braising:** Braising combines both wet and dry heat to tenderize meats and vegetables. Start by searing the ingredients in a hot pan, add liquid and cook slowly in a covered pot. This method makes flavorful dishes like braised lamb shanks, artichokes, and beef stew.

- **Marinating:** Marinating is essential for infusing meats, fish, and vegetables with flavor before cooking. A Mediterranean marinade typically includes olive oil, lemon juice, garlic, herbs, and spices. To ensure the tastes are absorbed, let the ingredients marinade for at least half an hour. This technique perfectly prepares dishes like marinated grilled chicken, seafood skewers, and vegetable kebabs.

- **Steaming:** Steaming is a nutrient-dense and naturally flavor-preserving cooking method. Use a steamer basket over boiling water to cook vegetables, fish, and dumplings. Steaming is ideal for steamed artichokes, fish fillets, and Mediterranean vegetable medleys.

- **Toasting:** Toasting nuts, seeds, and spices enhances their flavors and adds a rich, nutty aroma to dishes. Toast them in a dry skillet over medium heat, stirring often, until aromatic and golden brown. Toasting is perfect for ingredients like pine nuts for salads, cumin seeds for stews, and sesame seeds for dips.

Mastering these Mediterranean cooking techniques can help you create various flavorful and healthy dishes. These methods enhance the taste and presentation of your meals and highlight the simplicity and richness of Mediterranean cuisine. Impress your guests and elevate your cooking by incorporating these techniques into your culinary repertoire.

Tips for Efficient Meal Prep

A great method to make sure that tasty, nutritious Mediterranean meals are available all week long is to prepare your meals in advance. Here are some strategic tips to help you streamline your meal prep process, save time, and stay organized:

Plan Your Meals: Plan your meals for the upcoming week first. Decide on various dishes incorporating different ingredients to keep your diet balanced and exciting. Write down the meals you plan to make and the ingredients you will need. Consider incorporating snacks, dinner, lunch, and breakfast into your schedule.

Make a Shopping List: Make a comprehensive grocery list based on your food plan. Organize the list by grocery store sections (e.g., produce, dairy, grains) to make your shopping trip more efficient. Stick to the list to make sure you have everything and prevent impulsive buying.

Batch Cooking: Batch cooking is an effective way to prepare multiple meals at once. Select recipes that lend themselves to easy doubling or tripling, then prepare larger quantities. For example, you can make a big batch of soup, stew, or grains that can be portioned out and stored for the week.

Prep Ingredients in Advance: Set aside time to prep ingredients ahead of time. Wash and chop vegetables, marinate proteins, and portion out snacks. Prepped ingredients make it quicker and easier to assemble meals during the week.

Use Versatile Ingredients: Choose ingredients that work well in a variety of dishes. In this case, roasted veggies are a great addition to wraps, grain bowls, and salads. Grain bases, such as brown rice or quinoa, can be used for a number of dishes. This reduces the amount of prep work and ensures you use up all your ingredients.

Invest in Good Storage Containers: Invest in a collection of high-quality, dishwasher, and microwave-safe, and leak-proof storage containers. Clear containers allow you to see what's inside, making it easier to find what you need.

Label and Date Your Meals: Put the name of the dish and the preparation date on the label of every container. This will help you track how long each meal has been stored and ensure you consume the oldest meals first to reduce waste.

Utilize Freezer-Friendly Recipes: Make meals that are freezer-friendly so they can be kept for longer. Casseroles, soups, stews, and cooked grains freeze well and can be reheated quickly—portion these meals into individual servings before freezing for easy, grab-and-go options.

Cook Once, Eat Twice: Arrange dinners that have several uses as separate dishes. For example, grilled chicken can be used to wraps, salads, and grain bowls. You might be able to prepare fewer meals and have more variety using this strategy. It may also save you time.

Stay Organized: Keep your kitchen and pantry organized to make meal prep more efficient. Store similar items together, keep frequently used ingredients within easy reach, and maintain a tidy workspace. An organized kitchen makes it easier to find what you need and speeds up the cooking process.

Use Time-Saving Tools: Make use of time- and labor-saving kitchen appliances like a mandoline for speedy vegetable preparation, a food processor for chopping and slicing, and an instant pot or slow cooker for hands-off cooking. With the help of these instruments, preparing meals may be quicker and more fun.

Prioritize Nutrient-Dense Foods: Focus on preparing nutrient-dense foods that align with the Mediterranean Diet. Add a range of vibrant veggies, healthful grains, lean meats, and good fats. This ensures your meals are convenient and packed with essential nutrients.

These guidelines will help you quickly and easily cook nutritious Mediterranean-style meals that you can eat all week long. Efficient meal prep helps you save time, reduce stress, and stay committed to a nutritious and balanced diet.

How to Store Fresh Produce and Herbs

Storing fresh produce and herbs is crucial for maintaining flavor, texture, and nutritional value. Here are some strategic tips to help you store your fresh ingredients effectively, ensuring they stay fresh and last longer:

Storing Vegetables

- **Leafy Greens**

Storage Method: Wash and thoroughly dry leafy greens such as spinach, kale, and lettuce. After placing them in an airtight container or plastic bag, wrap them in a paper towel to absorb any remaining moisture.

Shelf Life: 5-7 days in the refrigerator.

- **Root Vegetables:**

Storage Method: Store root vegetables like carrots, potatoes, and beets in a cool, dark, and dry place. Remove greens from root vegetables to prevent them from drawing moisture from the roots.

Shelf Life: 2-4 weeks in a cool, dark place; 1-2 weeks in the refrigerator for some roots like carrots.

- **Bell Peppers and Cucumbers:**

Storage Method: Keep bell peppers and cucumbers in the crisper drawer of your refrigerator. To absorb moisture, store them in a paper towel-lined container or plastic bag.

Shelf Life: 1-2 weeks in the refrigerator.

- **Tomatoes:**

Storage Method: Store tomatoes at room temperature away from direct sunlight. Once fully ripe, you can refrigerate them to extend their shelf life, which may alter their texture.

Shelf Life: 3-7 days at room temperature; 1 week in the refrigerator once ripe.

- **Mushrooms:**

Storage Method: Keep mushrooms in a paper bag or wrap them in a paper towel inside a plastic bag. To avoid overly moistening them, wait to wash them right before using.

Shelf Life: 4-7 days in the refrigerator.

Storing Fruits

- **Berries:**

Storage Method: Store berries like strawberries, blueberries, and raspberries in their original container or a breathable container lined with paper towels. Do not wash until ready to eat.

Shelf Life: 3-7 days in the refrigerator.

- **Citrus Fruits:**

Storage Method: Keep citrus fruits such as oranges, lemons, and limes at room temperature or in the refrigerator crisper drawer. Store in a mesh bag to allow air circulation.

Shelf Life: 1-2 weeks at room temperature; up to 1 month in the refrigerator.

- **Apples and Pears:**

Storage Method: Store apples and pears in the crisper drawer of your refrigerator. Please keep them in a plastic bag with holes for ventilation.

Shelf Life: 3-4 weeks in the refrigerator.

- **Bananas:**

Storage Method: Store bananas at room temperature. To slow ripening, separate them and wrap the stems in plastic wrap.

Shelf Life: 2-7 days at room temperature.

Storing Herbs

- **Soft Herbs (Basil, Cilantro, Parsley):**

Storage Method: Trim the ends and place the herbs in a jar with a small amount of water, like a bouquet. Place a plastic bag over it loosely and refrigerate. For basil, keep at room temperature.

Shelf Life: 1-2 weeks.

- **Hard Herbs (Rosemary, Thyme, Sage):**

Storage Method: Place these herbs in an airtight container or plastic bag and refrigerate after wrapping them in a damp paper towel.

Shelf Life: 1-2 weeks.

- **Drying Herbs:**

Storage Method: The herbs should be tied into little bundles and hung upside down in a warm, dry place with good ventilation. After they have dried, keep them out of direct sunlight in an airtight container.

Shelf Life: Several months to a year.

General Tips

- Avoid Overcrowding: Ensure adequate airflow around your produce to prevent spoilage.

- Check Regularly: To stop spoiling from spreading to other food, regularly inspect your stored produce and discard any that exhibit any symptoms of deterioration.

- Use Perforated Bags: Store vegetables and fruits in perforated plastic bags, which allow air circulation while retaining moisture.

- Store Separately: Since some fruits release ethylene gas, which can hasten the ripening of surrounding veggies, store fruits and vegetables apart.

By following these tips, you can maximize the freshness and longevity of your produce and herbs, ensuring you always have high-quality ingredients for your Mediterranean meals.

Quick and Easy Mediterranean Cooking Hacks

Incorporating Mediterranean flavors and techniques into your daily cooking can be simple and efficient with a few intelligent hacks. Here are some tips to help you prepare delicious Mediterranean meals quickly and easily:

Use Pre-Chopped Vegetables

Hack: Purchase pre-chopped vegetables from the grocery store or spend some time prepping vegetables in bulk at the beginning of the week.

Benefit: It saves time during meal preparation and ensures you always have vegetables ready for salads, stir-fries, or snacks.

Marinate in Minutes

Hack: Use quick marinades to infuse flavor into meats, fish, and vegetables. Combine olive oil, lemon juice, garlic, and herbs for a simple and effective marinade.

Benefit: Enhances flavor without the need for long marinating times.

Make Use of Canned Goods

Hack: Keep various canned goods such as chickpeas, tomatoes, and olives. These ingredients can be quickly added to salads, stews, and pasta dishes.

Benefit: Provides convenience and speeds up meal preparation.

One-Pot Meals

Hack: Prepare one-pot Mediterranean dishes like vegetable and chickpea stew, lemon chicken with potatoes, or seafood paella.

Benefit: Reduces cleanup and simplifies cooking by using fewer dishes.

Quick Cooking Grains

Hack: Go for whole grains that cook quickly, such bulgur or quinoa. These grains can serve as a foundation for salads, bowls, and side dishes; they cook in around 15 minutes.

Benefit: Provides a nutritious and fast alternative to longer-cooking grains.

Sheet Pan Dinners

Hack: Create easy sheet-pan dinners by roasting vegetables, fish, or chicken on a single tray. Season with olive oil, herbs, and spices before roasting.

Benefit: Simplifies cooking and cleanup, allowing you to prepare a complete meal in one go.

Frozen Vegetables and Fruits

Hack: Keep frozen vegetables and fruits on hand for quick meal additions. Frozen spinach, peas, and mixed berries are exceptionally versatile.

Benefit: Ensures you always have nutritious ingredients, even when fresh produce runs out.

Quick Homemade Dressings

Hack: Whip up homemade dressings using essential pantry ingredients. To make a basic vinaigrette, combine honey, vinegar, mustard, and olive oil.

Benefit: Adds fresh, flavorful dressings to your salads and dishes in minutes.

Herb Ice Cubes

Hack: Use ice cube trays to freeze fresh herbs in olive oil or water. Pop a cube into your pan when cooking for instant flavor.

Benefit: Preserves herbs and provides a quick flavor boost for soups, stews, and sautés.

Use Leftovers Creatively

Hack: Repurpose leftovers into new meals. For example, use leftover roasted vegetables in a frittata, turn cooked grains into a salad, or add leftover meat to a wrap.

Benefit: Reduces food waste and makes meal preparation more efficient.

Pre-Made Spice Blends

Hack: Create or purchase pre-made Mediterranean spice blends such as za'atar, Italian seasoning, or herbes de Provence.

Benefit: Quickly season your dishes without measuring individual spices.

Quick-Pickled Vegetables

Hack: Make quick pickles by marinating vegetables like cucumbers, onions, and carrots in vinegar, water, sugar, and salt for at least an hour.

Benefit: Adds a tangy, crunchy element to your dishes with minimal effort.

You may enjoy the flavors and health advantages of the Mediterranean Diet without spending hours in the kitchen by implementing these simple and quick Mediterranean cooking hacks into your daily routine. These techniques make it simple and quick to make delicious meals, which makes eating a balanced diet more accessible and enjoyable.

CHAPTER 4

Breakfast

Greek Yogurt Breakfast Bowl

Ingredients:

- 1 cup Greek yogurt

- 1/2 cup mixed berries (strawberries, blueberries, raspberries)

- 1/4 cup granola

- 1 tablespoon honey

- 1 tablespoon chia seeds

- Fresh mint leaves (optional, for garnish)

Instructions:

1. Scoop the Greek yogurt into a bowl.

2. Top with mixed berries and granola.

3. Drizzle honey over the top.

4. Sprinkle with chia seeds.

5. Garnish with fresh mint leaves if desired.

How to Serve:

Serve immediately while the yogurt is chilled, ensuring the granola remains crunchy.

Nutrition Count per Serving:

Approximately: 300 calories, 10g fat, 40g carbs, 15g protein, 6g fiber, 20g sugar

Mediterranean Omelet

Ingredients:

- 3 large eggs

- 1/4 cup diced tomatoes

- 1/4 cup chopped spinach

- 1/4 cup crumbled feta cheese

- 1/4 cup diced red onion

- 1 tablespoon olive oil

- Salt and pepper to taste

Instructions:

1. In a medium bowl, whisk the eggs with a pinch of salt and pepper.

2. Heat olive oil in a non-stick skillet over medium heat.

3. Add the red onion and sauté until softened, about 2 minutes.

4. Add the tomatoes and spinach, and cook until spinach is wilted, about 1-2 minutes.

5. Pour the whisked eggs into the skillet, swirling to distribute evenly.

6. Sprinkle feta cheese on top.

7. Cook until the omelet is set, and the edges are slightly browned, about 3-4 minutes.

8. Fold the omelet in half and slide onto a plate.

How to Serve:

Serve hot, possibly with a side of whole grain toast or a small mixed salad.

Nutrition Count per Serving:

Approximately: 320 calories, 24g fat, 8g carbs, 18g protein, 2g fiber, 4g sugar

Bulgur Wheat Cereal with Apples and Almonds

Ingredients:

- 1 cup bulgur wheat

- 2 cups water

- 1 apple, diced

- 1/4 cup sliced almonds

- 1 tablespoon honey

- 1/2 teaspoon ground cinnamon

- 1/4 teaspoon ground nutmeg

- Pinch of salt

Instructions:

1. In a medium saucepan, bring the water to a boil.

2. Stir in the bulgur wheat and a pinch of salt.

3. Reduce heat to low, cover, and simmer for 12-15 minutes or until bulgur is tender and water is absorbed.

4. In a small bowl, mix the diced apple with ground cinnamon and nutmeg.

5. Once the bulgur is cooked, stir in the apple mixture and honey.

6. Top with sliced almonds.

How to Serve:

Serve warm, optionally with a splash of milk or a dollop of yogurt.

Nutrition Count per Serving:

Approximately: 250 calories, 6g fat, 45g carbs, 6g protein, 8g fiber, 15g sugar

Ricotta and Fruit Bruschetta

Ingredients:

- 4 slices whole-grain baguette

- 1/2 cup ricotta cheese

- 1/2 cup mixed fresh fruit (e.g., strawberries, blueberries, peaches), diced

- 1 tablespoon honey

- Fresh mint leaves (optional, for garnish)

Instructions:

1. Toast the baguette slices until golden brown.

2. Spread ricotta cheese evenly over each slice.

3. Top with diced fresh fruit.

4. Drizzle honey over the top.

5. Garnish with fresh mint leaves if desired.

How to Serve:

Serve immediately while the baguette slices are still warm and crispy.

Nutrition Count per Serving:

Approximately: 200 calories, 6g fat, 28g carbs, 8g protein, 4g fiber, 10g sugar

Savory Feta, Spinach, and Red Pepper Muffins

Ingredients:

- 1 cup whole wheat flour
- 1/2 cup feta cheese, crumbled
- 1 cup fresh spinach, chopped
- 1/2 cup red bell pepper, diced
- 2 large eggs
- 1/2 cup milk
- 1/4 cup olive oil
- 1 teaspoon baking powder
- 1/2 teaspoon baking soda
- 1/4 teaspoon salt
- 1/4 teaspoon black pepper

Instructions:

1. Preheat the oven to 375°F (190°C) and grease a muffin tin.
2. In a large bowl, whisk together the flour, baking powder, baking soda, salt, and black pepper.
3. In another bowl, beat the eggs and then stir in the milk and olive oil.
4. Add the wet ingredients to the dry ingredients and mix until just combined.
5. Fold in the feta cheese, spinach, and red bell pepper.
6. Divide the batter evenly among the muffin tin cups.
7. Bake for 20-25 minutes, or until a toothpick inserted into the center comes out clean.
8. Allow it to cool slightly before serving.

How to Serve:

Serve warm, perfect for a quick breakfast on the go or a savory snack.

Nutrition Count per Serving:

Approximately: 180 calories, 10g fat, 15g carbs, 6g protein, 2g fiber, 2g sugar

Oatmeal with Figs, Almonds, and Chia Seeds

Ingredients:

- 1 cup rolled oats

- 2 cups water or milk (or a combination of both)

- 1/4 cup dried figs, chopped

- 2 tablespoons almonds, sliced

- 1 tablespoon chia seeds

- 1 tablespoon honey or maple syrup (optional)

- 1/2 teaspoon ground cinnamon

- Pinch of salt

Instructions:

1. In a medium saucepan, bring the water or milk to a boil.

2. Stir in the oats, chopped figs, and a pinch of salt.

3. Reduce heat to low and cook, stirring occasionally, until the oats are tender and the mixture is creamy, about 5-7 minutes.

4. Remove from heat and stir in the chia seeds, cinnamon, and honey or maple syrup if using.

5. Top with sliced almonds.

How to Serve:

Serve warm, optionally with an additional drizzle of honey or maple syrup.

Nutrition Count per Serving:

Approximately: 300 calories, 10g fat, 50g carbs, 8g protein, 8g fiber, 20g sugar

Banana Almond Oatmeal Smoothie

Ingredients:

- 1 banana

- 1/2 cup rolled oats

- 1 tablespoon almond butter

- 1 cup almond milk (or any milk of your choice)

- 1 tablespoon honey (optional)

- 1/2 teaspoon ground cinnamon

- Ice cubes (optional)

Instructions:

1. In a blender, combine the banana, rolled oats, almond butter, almond milk, honey (if using), and ground cinnamon.

2. Blend until smooth.

3. Add ice cubes if you prefer a colder smoothie and blend again until the ice is crushed.

How to Serve:

Pour into a glass and serve immediately. Garnish with a sprinkle of cinnamon or a few almond slices if desired.

Nutrition Count per Serving:

Approximately: 250 calories, 8g fat, 40g carbs, 6g protein, 5g fiber, 15g sugar

Apricot and Hazelnut Smoothie

Ingredients:

- 1 cup dried apricots, soaked in water overnight and drained

- 1/4 cup hazelnuts

- 1 cup Greek yogurt

- 1 cup orange juice

- 1 tablespoon honey (optional)

- Ice cubes (optional)

Instructions:

1. In a blender, combine the soaked apricots, hazelnuts, Greek yogurt, and orange juice.

2. Blend until smooth.

3. Add honey and ice cubes if desired and blend again until the ice is crushed.

How to Serve:

Pour into a glass and serve immediately. Garnish with a few chopped hazelnuts or a slice of apricot if desired.

Nutrition Count per Serving:

Approximately: 300 calories, 10g fat, 45g carbs, 8g protein, 6g fiber, 30g sugar

Green Detox Juice

Ingredients:

- 1 cucumber, chopped

- 2 celery stalks, chopped

- 1 green apple, cored and chopped

- 1 cup spinach leaves

- 1/2 lemon, juiced

- 1-inch piece of ginger, peeled and chopped

- 1 cup water

Instructions:

1. In a blender, combine the cucumber, celery, green apple, spinach leaves, lemon juice, ginger, and water.

2. Blend until smooth.

3. Strain the juice through a fine-mesh sieve or cheesecloth to remove the pulp, if desired.

How to Serve:

Serve immediately over ice or chilled.

Nutrition Count per Serving:

Approximately: 120 calories, 0g fat, 30g carbs, 2g protein, 5g fiber, 15g sugar

Citrus Carrot Juice

Ingredients:

- 4 large carrots, peeled and chopped

- 2 oranges, peeled and segmented

- 1 lemon, peeled

- 1-inch piece of ginger, peeled

- 1 cup water

Instructions:

1. In a blender, combine the carrots, oranges, lemon, ginger, and water.

2. Blend until smooth.

3. Strain the juice through a fine-mesh sieve or cheesecloth to remove the pulp, if desired.

How to Serve:

Serve immediately over ice or chilled.

Nutrition Count per Serving:

Approximately: 150 calories, 0g fat, 35g carbs, 3g protein, 7g fiber, 20g sugar

Tomato and Feta Frittata

Ingredients:

- 6 large eggs

- 1/4 cup milk

- 1 cup cherry tomatoes, halved

- 1/2 cup crumbled feta cheese

- 1/4 cup chopped fresh basil

- 1 tablespoon olive oil

- Salt and pepper to taste

Instructions:

1. Preheat the oven to 375°F (190°C).

2. In a medium bowl, whisk together the eggs, milk, salt, and pepper.

3. Heat olive oil in an oven-safe skillet over medium heat.

4. Add the cherry tomatoes and cook for 2-3 minutes until slightly softened.

5. Pour the egg mixture into the skillet and cook for 2-3 minutes until the edges start to set.

6. Sprinkle feta cheese and chopped basil over the top.

7. Transfer the skillet to the oven and bake for 10-15 minutes, or until the frittata is set and lightly golden.

How to Serve:

Serve warm, cut into wedges. Perfect with a side salad or whole grain bread.

Nutrition Count per Serving:

Approximately: 250 calories, 18g fat, 5g carbs, 16g protein, 1g fiber, 3g sugar

Bell Pepper and Onion Scramble

Ingredients:

- 3 large eggs

- 1/4 cup diced red bell pepper

- 1/4 cup diced green bell pepper

- 1/4 cup diced onion

- 1 tablespoon olive oil

- Salt and pepper to taste

Instructions:

1. In a medium bowl, whisk the eggs with a pinch of salt and pepper.

2. Heat olive oil in a non-stick skillet over medium heat.

3. Add the diced bell peppers and onion, and cook until softened, about 3-4 minutes.

4. Pour the whisked eggs into the skillet and cook, stirring gently, until the eggs are scrambled and cooked through.

How to Serve:

Serve hot, possibly with a side of whole grain toast or a small mixed salad.

Nutrition Count per Serving:

Approximately: 200 calories, 14g fat, 6g carbs, 12g protein, 2g fiber, 3g sugar

Avocado Toast with Cherry Tomatoes

Ingredients:

- 2 slices whole grain bread

- 1 ripe avocado

- 1/2 cup cherry tomatoes, halved

- 1 tablespoon olive oil

- 1 teaspoon lemon juice

- Salt and pepper to taste

- Red pepper flakes (optional)

Instructions:

1. Toast the slices of whole grain bread until golden brown.

2. In a small bowl, mash the avocado with lemon juice, salt, and pepper.

3. Spread the mashed avocado evenly over the toasted bread.

4. Top with halved cherry tomatoes.

5. Drizzle olive oil over the top and sprinkle with red pepper flakes if desired.

How to Serve:

Serve immediately as a nutritious breakfast or snack.

Nutrition Count per Serving:

Approximately: 350 calories, 20g fat, 35g carbs, 7g protein, 9g fiber, 3g sugar

Almond Butter and Banana Smoothie

Ingredients:

- 1 banana

- 1 tablespoon almond butter

- 1 cup almond milk (or any milk of your choice)

- 1 tablespoon honey (optional)

- 1/2 teaspoon ground cinnamon

- Ice cubes (optional)

Instructions:

1. In a blender, combine the banana, almond butter, almond milk, honey (if using), and ground cinnamon.

2. Blend until smooth.

3. Add ice cubes if you prefer a colder smoothie and blend again until the ice is crushed.

How to Serve:

Pour into a glass and serve immediately. Garnish with a sprinkle of cinnamon or a few almond slices if desired.

Nutrition Count per Serving:

Approximately: 250 calories, 10g fat, 35g carbs, 5g protein, 4g fiber, 15g sugar

Blueberry and Walnut Oatmeal

Ingredients:

- 1 cup rolled oats

- 2 cups water or milk (or a combination of both)

- 1/2 cup fresh blueberries

- 1/4 cup chopped walnuts

- 1 tablespoon honey or maple syrup (optional)

- 1/2 teaspoon ground cinnamon

- Pinch of salt

Instructions:

1. In a medium saucepan, bring the water or milk to a boil.

2. Stir in the oats and a pinch of salt.

3. Reduce heat to low and cook, stirring occasionally, until the oats are tender and the mixture is creamy, about 5-7 minutes.

4. Remove from heat and stir in the blueberries, chopped walnuts, cinnamon, and honey or maple syrup if using.

How to Serve:

Serve warm, optionally with an additional drizzle of honey or maple syrup.

Nutrition Count per Serving:

Approximately: 350 calories, 12g fat, 50g carbs, 8g protein, 7g fiber, 15g sugar

CHAPTER 5

Lunch

Greek Chicken Salad

Ingredients:

- 2 cups cooked chicken breast, shredded
- 1 cup cherry tomatoes, halved
- 1 cucumber, diced
- 1/4 red onion, thinly sliced
- 1/2 cup Kalamata olives, pitted and halved
- 1/2 cup feta cheese, crumbled
- 2 cups mixed greens
- 1/4 cup extra virgin olive oil
- 2 tablespoons red wine vinegar
- 1 teaspoon dried oregano
- Salt and pepper to taste

Instructions:

1. In a large bowl, combine the shredded chicken, cherry tomatoes, cucumber, red onion, Kalamata olives, feta cheese, and mixed greens.
2. In a small bowl, whisk together the olive oil, red wine vinegar, dried oregano, salt, and pepper.
3. Pour the dressing over the salad and toss to combine.

How to Serve:

Serve immediately, garnished with additional feta cheese and olives if desired.

Nutrition Count per Serving:

Approximately: 400 calories, 28g fat, 10g carbs, 28g protein, 4g fiber, 5g sugar

Mediterranean Tuna Salad

Ingredients:

- 2 cans tuna in water, drained
- 1/2 cup cherry tomatoes, halved
- 1/2 cucumber, diced
- 1/4 red onion, finely chopped
- 1/4 cup Kalamata olives, pitted and chopped
- 1/4 cup feta cheese, crumbled
- 2 tablespoons capers, rinsed and drained
- 2 tablespoons fresh parsley, chopped
- 3 tablespoons extra virgin olive oil
- 1 tablespoon lemon juice
- Salt and pepper to taste

Instructions:

1. In a large bowl, combine the drained tuna, cherry tomatoes, cucumber, red onion, Kalamata olives, feta cheese, capers, and fresh parsley.

2. In a small bowl, whisk together the olive oil, lemon juice, salt, and pepper.

3. Pour the dressing over the salad and toss to combine.

How to Serve:

Serve immediately, optionally on a bed of mixed greens or in a pita pocket.

Nutrition Count per Serving:

Approximately: 300 calories, 20g fat, 6g carbs, 24g protein, 2g fiber, 3g sugar

Falafel Wraps

Ingredients:

- 1 cup canned chickpeas, rinsed and drained
- 1/4 cup chopped onion
- 2 cloves garlic, minced
- 1/4 cup fresh parsley, chopped
- 1 teaspoon ground cumin
- 1 teaspoon ground coriander
- 1/2 teaspoon baking powder
- 2 tablespoons all-purpose flour
- Salt and pepper to taste
- 2 tablespoons olive oil
- 4 whole wheat wraps
- 1 cup mixed greens
- 1/2 cup cherry tomatoes, halved
- 1/2 cup cucumber, sliced
- 1/4 cup tahini sauce

Instructions:

1. In a food processor, combine the chickpeas, onion, garlic, parsley, cumin, coriander, baking powder, flour, salt, and pepper. Pulse until the mixture is finely ground but not pureed.
2. Form the mixture into small patties.
3. Heat the olive oil in a skillet over medium heat. Fry the patties until golden brown, about 3-4 minutes per side.
4. Warm the whole wheat wraps in a dry skillet or microwave.
5. Fill each wrap with mixed greens, cherry tomatoes, cucumber, and falafel patties. Drizzle with tahini sauce.

How to Serve:

Serve immediately, rolled up and cut in half if desired.

Nutrition Count per Serving:

Approximately: 350 calories, 14g fat, 45g carbs, 12g protein, 10g fiber, 4g sugar

Grilled Vegetable Panini

Ingredients:

- 1 zucchini, sliced
- 1 red bell pepper, sliced
- 1 yellow bell pepper, sliced
- 1 eggplant, sliced
- 1/4 cup olive oil
- 1 teaspoon dried oregano
- Salt and pepper to taste
- 4 slices whole grain bread
- 4 slices mozzarella cheese
- 1/4 cup pesto sauce

Instructions:

1. Preheat a grill or grill pan over medium-high heat.

2. In a bowl, toss the zucchini, bell peppers, and eggplant with olive oil, oregano, salt, and pepper.

3. Grill the vegetables until tender and lightly charred, about 3-4 minutes per side.

4. Spread pesto sauce on one side of each bread slice.

5. Layer grilled vegetables and mozzarella cheese between the bread slices, with the pesto sides facing in.

6. Grill the panini until the bread is golden brown and the cheese is melted, about 3-4 minutes per side.

How to Serve:

Serve immediately, optionally with a side salad or chips.

Nutrition Count per Serving:

Approximately: 400 calories, 20g fat, 40g carbs, 15g protein, 6g fiber, 5g sugar

Pita with Hummus and Veggies

Ingredients:

- 4 whole wheat pita breads

- 1 cup hummus

- 1 cucumber, sliced

- 1 red bell pepper, sliced

- 1 yellow bell pepper, sliced

- 1/2 cup cherry tomatoes, halved

- 1/4 cup Kalamata olives, pitted and halved

- 1/4 cup crumbled feta cheese

- Fresh parsley for garnish

Instructions:

1. Warm the pita breads in a dry skillet or microwave.

2. Spread a generous amount of hummus on each pita.

3. Top with cucumber slices, bell pepper slices, cherry tomatoes, Kalamata olives, and crumbled feta cheese.

4. Garnish with fresh parsley.

How to Serve:

Serve immediately as a refreshing and nutritious lunch option.

Nutrition Count per Serving:

Approximately: 350 calories, 14g fat, 45g carbs, 10g protein, 8g fiber, 6g sugar

Stuffed Portobello Mushrooms

Ingredients:

- 4 large Portobello mushrooms

- 1 cup cherry tomatoes, halved

- 1/2 cup spinach, chopped

- 1/2 cup feta cheese, crumbled

- 1/4 cup breadcrumbs

- 2 cloves garlic, minced

- 2 tablespoons olive oil

- Salt and pepper to taste

Instructions:

1. Preheat the oven to 375°F (190°C).

2. Clean the Portobello mushrooms and remove the stems.

3. In a bowl, combine the cherry tomatoes, spinach, feta cheese, breadcrumbs, garlic, olive oil, salt, and pepper.

4. Stuff each mushroom cap with the mixture.

5. Place the stuffed mushrooms on a baking sheet and bake for 20-25 minutes, or until the mushrooms are tender and the topping is golden brown.

How to Serve:

Serve warm, optionally with a side of mixed greens or a light salad.

Nutrition Count per Serving:

Approximately: 250 calories, 16g fat, 20g carbs, 8g protein, 4g fiber, 4g sugar

Stuffed Zucchini Boats

Ingredients:

- 4 medium zucchinis, halved lengthwise and seeds scooped out

- 1 cup cooked quinoa

- 1/2 cup cherry tomatoes, diced

- 1/4 cup red onion, finely chopped

- 1/2 cup crumbled feta cheese

- 2 tablespoons fresh parsley, chopped

- 1 tablespoon olive oil

- 1 teaspoon dried oregano

- Salt and pepper to taste

Instructions:

1. Preheat the oven to 375°F (190°C).

2. Arrange the zucchini halves on a baking sheet.

3. In a large bowl, mix together the cooked quinoa, cherry tomatoes, red onion, feta cheese, parsley, olive oil, oregano, salt, and pepper.

4. Spoon the mixture evenly into the zucchini halves.

5. Bake for 20-25 minutes, or until the zucchinis are tender and the filling is heated through.

How to Serve:

Serve warm, optionally garnished with extra parsley and a side of mixed greens.

Nutrition Count per Serving:

Approximately: 200 calories, 10g fat, 20g carbs, 6g protein, 4g fiber, 5g sugar

Spinach and Feta Quesadilla

Ingredients:

- 4 whole wheat tortillas

- 1 cup fresh spinach, chopped

- 1/2 cup crumbled feta cheese

- 1/2 cup shredded mozzarella cheese

- 1 tablespoon olive oil

- 1/2 teaspoon dried oregano

- Salt and pepper to taste

Instructions:

1. Heat olive oil in a large skillet over medium heat.

2. Place one tortilla in the skillet and sprinkle with half of the chopped spinach, feta cheese, mozzarella cheese, oregano, salt, and pepper.

3. Top with another tortilla and cook until the bottom tortilla is golden brown, about 2-3 minutes.

4. Carefully flip the quesadilla and cook until the other side is golden brown and the cheese is melted, another 2-3 minutes.

5. Repeat with the remaining tortillas and filling.

How to Serve:

Serve immediately, cut into wedges. Perfect with a side of salsa or Greek yogurt.

Nutrition Count per Serving:

Approximately: 300 calories, 16g fat, 28g carbs, 12g protein, 4g fiber, 2g sugar

Grilled Shrimp Skewers

Ingredients:

- 1 pound large shrimp, peeled and deveined

- 2 tablespoons olive oil

- 2 tablespoons lemon juice

- 2 cloves garlic, minced

- 1 teaspoon dried oregano

- Salt and pepper to taste

- Lemon wedges (for serving)

Instructions:

1. Preheat a grill or grill pan over medium-high heat.

2. In a bowl, mix together the olive oil, lemon juice, garlic, oregano, salt, and pepper.

3. Add the shrimp to the bowl and toss to coat evenly.

4. Thread the shrimp onto skewers.

5. Grill the shrimp skewers for 2-3 minutes per side, or until the shrimp are opaque and cooked through.

How to Serve:

Serve immediately with lemon wedges and optionally over a bed of quinoa or a light salad.

Nutrition Count per Serving:

Approximately: 200 calories, 10g fat, 2g carbs, 24g protein, 1g fiber, 0g sugar

Chickpea and Avocado Sandwich

Ingredients:

- 1 can chickpeas, drained and rinsed

- 1 ripe avocado

- 1 tablespoon lemon juice

- 1/4 cup red onion, finely chopped

- 1/4 cup fresh parsley, chopped

- Salt and pepper to taste

- 4 slices whole grain bread

- Mixed greens for garnish

Instructions:

1. In a medium bowl, mash the chickpeas and avocado together until well combined.

2. Stir in the lemon juice, red onion, parsley, salt, and pepper.

3. Toast the whole grain bread slices until golden brown.

4. Spread the chickpea and avocado mixture evenly on two slices of bread.

5. Top with mixed greens and place the remaining bread slices on top to form sandwiches.

How to Serve:

Serve immediately as a nutritious and filling lunch option.

Nutrition Count per Serving:

Approximately: 350 calories, 15g fat, 45g carbs, 10g protein, 10g fiber, 4g sugar

Roasted Red Pepper and Hummus Wrap

Ingredients:

- 4 whole wheat wraps

- 1 cup hummus

- 2 roasted red peppers, sliced

- 1 cup spinach leaves

- 1/2 cup shredded carrots

- 1/4 cup crumbled feta cheese

- 2 tablespoons olive oil

- Salt and pepper to taste

Instructions:

1. Spread a generous amount of hummus on each whole wheat wrap.

2. Layer with sliced roasted red peppers, spinach leaves, shredded carrots, and crumbled feta cheese.

3. Drizzle with olive oil and season with salt and pepper.

4. Roll up each wrap tightly and cut in half if desired.

How to Serve:

Serve immediately as a light and flavorful lunch.

Nutrition Count per Serving:

Approximately: 300 calories, 14g fat, 35g carbs, 8g protein, 8g fiber, 6g sugar

Lentil and Quinoa Patties

Ingredients:

- 1 cup cooked lentils
- 1 cup cooked quinoa
- 1/4 cup breadcrumbs
- 1/4 cup grated carrot
- 1/4 cup finely chopped onion
- 2 cloves garlic, minced
- 1 tablespoon fresh parsley, chopped
- 1 egg, beaten
- 1 tablespoon olive oil
- Salt and pepper to taste

Instructions:

1. In a large bowl, combine the cooked lentils, cooked quinoa, breadcrumbs, grated carrot, chopped onion, garlic, parsley, beaten egg, salt, and pepper. Mix well.

2. Form the mixture into small patties.

3. Heat the olive oil in a skillet over medium heat.

4. Cook the patties for 3-4 minutes on each side, or until golden brown and crispy.

How to Serve:

Serve warm, optionally with a side of yogurt sauce or a mixed green salad.

Nutrition Count per Serving:

Approximately: 250 calories, 8g fat, 35g carbs, 10g protein, 6g fiber, 3g sugar

Chicken and Spinach Salad

Ingredients:

- 2 cups cooked chicken breast, shredded

- 4 cups fresh spinach leaves

- 1/2 cup cherry tomatoes, halved

- 1/4 cup red onion, thinly sliced

- 1/4 cup crumbled feta cheese

- 1/4 cup walnuts, chopped

- 2 tablespoons olive oil

- 1 tablespoon balsamic vinegar

- Salt and pepper to taste

Instructions:

1. In a large salad bowl, combine the shredded chicken, spinach leaves, cherry tomatoes, red onion, feta cheese, and walnuts.

2. In a small bowl, whisk together the olive oil, balsamic vinegar, salt, and pepper.

3. Drizzle the dressing over the salad and toss to combine.

How to Serve:

Serve immediately, optionally with whole grain bread or a light soup.

Nutrition Count per Serving:

Approximately: 350 calories, 20g fat, 10g carbs, 30g protein, 4g fiber, 4g sugar

Couscous and Roasted Vegetable Bowl

Ingredients:

- 1 cup couscous
- 2 cups vegetable broth
- 1 zucchini, diced
- 1 red bell pepper, diced
- 1 yellow bell pepper, diced
- 1 red onion, diced
- 2 tablespoons olive oil
- 1 teaspoon dried thyme
- 1 teaspoon dried oregano
- Salt and pepper to taste
- 1/4 cup crumbled feta cheese
- 2 tablespoons fresh parsley, chopped

Instructions:

1. Preheat the oven to 400°F (200°C).
2. In a large bowl, toss the diced zucchini, red bell pepper, yellow bell pepper, and red onion with olive oil, thyme, oregano, salt, and pepper.
3. Spread the vegetables on a baking sheet and roast for 20-25 minutes, or until tender and slightly caramelized.
4. Meanwhile, bring the vegetable broth to a boil in a medium saucepan. Stir in the couscous, cover, and remove from heat. Let sit for 5 minutes, then fluff with a fork.
5. In a large bowl, combine the cooked couscous, roasted vegetables, feta cheese, and fresh parsley.

How to Serve:

Serve warm or at room temperature, optionally with a side of mixed greens.

Nutrition Count per Serving:

Approximately: 300 calories, 12g fat, 40g carbs, 8g protein, 6g fiber, 8g sugar

Tuna and Roasted Vegetable Bowl

Ingredients:

- 1 can tuna in water, drained

- 1 cup cooked quinoa

- 1 zucchini, diced

- 1 red bell pepper, diced

- 1 yellow bell pepper, diced

- 1 red onion, diced

- 2 tablespoons olive oil

- 1 teaspoon dried thyme

- 1 teaspoon dried oregano

- Salt and pepper to taste

- 2 tablespoons fresh parsley, chopped

Instructions:

1. Preheat the oven to 400°F (200°C).

2. In a large bowl, toss the diced zucchini, red bell pepper, yellow bell pepper, and red onion with olive oil, thyme, oregano, salt, and pepper.

3. Spread the vegetables on a baking sheet and roast for 20-25 minutes, or until tender and slightly caramelized.

4. In a large bowl, combine the drained tuna, cooked quinoa, roasted vegetables, and fresh parsley.

How to Serve:

Serve warm or at room temperature, optionally with a drizzle of olive oil or lemon juice.

Nutrition Count per Serving:

Approximately: 350 calories, 14g fat, 35g carbs, 20g protein, 6g fiber, 7g sugar

CHAPTER 6

Snacks and Appetizers

Bread with Herb Curd

Ingredients:

- 1 loaf whole grain bread, sliced

- 1 cup curd (Greek yogurt or strained yogurt)

- 1 tablespoon fresh parsley, chopped

- 1 tablespoon fresh dill, chopped

- 1 clove garlic, minced

- Salt and pepper to taste

- 1 tablespoon olive oil

Instructions:

1. In a medium bowl, combine the curd, parsley, dill, minced garlic, salt, and pepper. Mix well.

2. Toast the whole grain bread slices until golden brown.

3. Spread the herb curd mixture evenly over each slice of toast.

4. Drizzle with a bit of olive oil.

How to Serve:

Serve immediately as a light snack or appetizer.

Nutrition Count per Serving:

Approximately: 150 calories, 5g fat, 20g carbs, 6g protein, 3g fiber, 2g sugar

Bell Peppers Stuffed with Feta and Dill

Ingredients:

- 4 bell peppers (red, yellow, or green), halved and seeds removed

- 1 cup feta cheese, crumbled

- 1/4 cup fresh dill, chopped

- 1/4 cup fresh parsley, chopped

- 1 clove garlic, minced

- 1 tablespoon olive oil

- Salt and pepper to taste

Instructions:

1. Preheat the oven to 375°F (190°C).

2. In a medium bowl, mix together the feta cheese, dill, parsley, minced garlic, olive oil, salt, and pepper.

3. Stuff each bell pepper half with the feta mixture.

4. Place the stuffed bell peppers on a baking sheet and bake for 20-25 minutes, or until the peppers are tender and the stuffing is golden brown.

How to Serve:

Serve warm as an appetizer or side dish.

Nutrition Count per Serving:

Approximately: 200 calories, 14g fat, 10g carbs, 6g protein, 3g fiber, 4g sugar

Avocado and Lime Guacamole

Ingredients:

- 2 ripe avocados

- 1 small red onion, finely chopped

- 1 small tomato, diced

- 1 clove garlic, minced

- 1 lime, juiced

- 1/4 cup fresh cilantro, chopped

- Salt and pepper to taste

Instructions:

1. In a medium bowl, mash the avocados with a fork until smooth.

2. Stir in the red onion, tomato, minced garlic, lime juice, cilantro, salt, and pepper.

3. Mix until well combined.

How to Serve:

Serve immediately with whole grain tortilla chips or vegetable sticks.

Nutrition Count per Serving:

Approximately: 150 calories, 10g fat, 15g carbs, 2g protein, 6g fiber, 2g sugar

Roasted Chickpeas

Ingredients:

- 1 can chickpeas, drained and rinsed

- 1 tablespoon olive oil

- 1 teaspoon paprika

- 1/2 teaspoon garlic powder

- 1/2 teaspoon ground cumin

- Salt and pepper to taste

Instructions:

1. Preheat the oven to 400°F (200°C).

2. Pat the chickpeas dry with a paper towel.

3. In a large bowl, toss the chickpeas with olive oil, paprika, garlic powder, ground cumin, salt, and pepper.

4. Spread the chickpeas on a baking sheet in a single layer.

5. Roast for 20-30 minutes, or until the chickpeas are crispy, shaking the pan halfway through.

How to Serve:

Serve warm or at room temperature as a crunchy snack.

Nutrition Count per Serving:

Approximately: 120 calories, 5g fat, 15g carbs, 5g protein, 4g fiber, 1g sugar

Stuffed Grape Leaves

Ingredients:

- 1 jar grape leaves, rinsed and drained
- 1 cup cooked rice
- 1/2 cup fresh dill, chopped
- 1/2 cup fresh parsley, chopped
- 1/4 cup pine nuts
- 1/4 cup currants or raisins
- 1 lemon, juiced
- 1/4 cup olive oil
- Salt and pepper to taste

Instructions:

1. In a large bowl, combine the cooked rice, dill, parsley, pine nuts, currants or raisins, lemon juice, olive oil, salt, and pepper.

2. Lay a grape leaf flat, vein side up, and place a tablespoon of the rice mixture near the stem end.

3. Fold in the sides of the leaf and roll up tightly to enclose the filling.

4. Repeat with the remaining grape leaves and filling.

5. Arrange the stuffed grape leaves in a large pot, seam side down.

6. Add enough water to cover the grape leaves and place a plate on top to keep them submerged.

7. Simmer over low heat for 30-40 minutes, or until the grape leaves are tender.

How to Serve:

Serve chilled or at room temperature as an appetizer.

Nutrition Count per Serving:

Approximately: 200 calories, 10g fat, 25g carbs, 4g protein, 3g fiber, 5g sugar

Hummus with Veggies

Ingredients:

- 1 can chickpeas, drained and rinsed

- 1/4 cup tahini

- 2 tablespoons olive oil

- 2 cloves garlic, minced

- 1 lemon, juiced

- 1/2 teaspoon ground cumin

- Salt and pepper to taste

- 1/4 cup water (as needed for consistency)

- Assorted fresh vegetables (carrot sticks, cucumber slices, bell pepper strips, cherry tomatoes)

Instructions:

1. In a food processor, combine the chickpeas, tahini, olive oil, minced garlic, lemon juice, ground cumin, salt, and pepper.

2. Blend until smooth, adding water as needed to reach desired consistency.

3. Transfer to a serving bowl.

How to Serve:

Serve with assorted fresh vegetables for dipping.

Nutrition Count per Serving:

Approximately: 150 calories, 8g fat, 15g carbs, 4g protein, 4g fiber, 2g sugar

Greek Yogurt Dip with Cucumber

Ingredients:

- 1 cup Greek yogurt

- 1 cucumber, grated and excess water squeezed out

- 1 clove garlic, minced

- 1 tablespoon fresh dill, chopped

- 1 tablespoon fresh mint, chopped

- 1 tablespoon olive oil

- 1 tablespoon lemon juice

- Salt and pepper to taste

Instructions:

1. In a medium bowl, combine the Greek yogurt, grated cucumber, minced garlic, dill, mint, olive oil, lemon juice, salt, and pepper.

2. Mix well until all ingredients are evenly distributed.

How to Serve:

Serve chilled with pita bread, crackers, or vegetable sticks.

Nutrition Count per Serving:

Approximately: 100 calories, 4g fat, 8g carbs, 6g protein, 1g fiber, 3g sugar

Zucchini Fritters

Ingredients:

- 2 medium zucchinis, grated
- 1/4 cup onion, finely chopped
- 1/4 cup feta cheese, crumbled
- 1/4 cup all-purpose flour
- 1 egg, beaten
- 1 clove garlic, minced
- 1 tablespoon fresh parsley, chopped
- 1/4 teaspoon baking powder
- Salt and pepper to taste
- Olive oil for frying

Instructions:

1. In a large bowl, combine the grated zucchini, chopped onion, feta cheese, flour, beaten egg, minced garlic, parsley, baking powder, salt, and pepper.

2. Mix until well combined.

3. Heat olive oil in a large skillet over medium heat.

4. Drop spoonful's of the zucchini mixture into the skillet and flatten slightly with a spatula.

5. Cook for 3-4 minutes per side, or until golden brown and crispy.

6. Transfer to a paper towel-lined plate to drain excess oil.

How to Serve:

Serve warm with a dollop of Greek yogurt or a squeeze of lemon.

Nutrition Count per Serving:

Approximately: 200 calories, 12g fat, 15g carbs, 6g protein, 2g fiber, 3g sugar

Spinach and Feta Stuffed Mushrooms

Ingredients:

- 12 large button mushrooms, stems removed

- 1 cup fresh spinach, chopped

- 1/2 cup feta cheese, crumbled

- 1/4 cup breadcrumbs

- 1 clove garlic, minced

- 1 tablespoon olive oil

- Salt and pepper to taste

Instructions:

1. Preheat the oven to 375°F (190°C).

2. In a medium bowl, combine the chopped spinach, feta cheese, breadcrumbs, minced garlic, olive oil, salt, and pepper.

3. Stuff each mushroom cap with the spinach mixture.

4. Place the stuffed mushrooms on a baking sheet.

5. Bake for 20-25 minutes, or until the mushrooms are tender and the stuffing is golden brown.

How to Serve:

Serve warm as an appetizer or snack.

Nutrition Count per Serving:

Approximately: 150 calories, 10g fat, 10g carbs, 6g protein, 2g fiber, 2g sugar

Tomato Bruschetta

Ingredients:

- 1 baguette, sliced into 1/2-inch thick slices

- 2 cups cherry tomatoes, diced

- 1/4 cup fresh basil, chopped

- 2 cloves garlic, minced

- 2 tablespoons balsamic vinegar

- 2 tablespoons olive oil

- Salt and pepper to taste

Instructions:

1. Preheat the oven to 400°F (200°C).

2. Arrange the baguette slices on a baking sheet and toast in the oven for 5-7 minutes, or until golden brown.

3. In a medium bowl, combine the diced tomatoes, chopped basil, minced garlic, balsamic vinegar, olive oil, salt, and pepper.

4. Spoon the tomato mixture onto each toasted baguette slice.

How to Serve:

Serve immediately as a fresh and flavorful appetizer.

Nutrition Count per Serving:

Approximately: 120 calories, 5g fat, 15g carbs, 3g protein, 1g fiber, 3g sugar

CHAPTER 7

Dinner

Baked Salmon with Herbs

Ingredients:

- 4 salmon fillets

- 2 tablespoons olive oil

- 2 cloves garlic, minced

- 1 lemon, thinly sliced

- 1 tablespoon fresh dill, chopped

- 1 tablespoon fresh parsley, chopped

- Salt and pepper to taste

Instructions:

1. Preheat the oven to 375°F (190°C).

2. Place the salmon fillets on a baking sheet lined with parchment paper.

3. Drizzle olive oil over the salmon and rub with minced garlic.

4. Season with salt and pepper.

5. Top each fillet with lemon slices and sprinkle with fresh dill and parsley.

6. Bake for 20-25 minutes, or until the salmon is cooked through and flakes easily with a fork.

How to Serve:

Serve warm with a side of steamed vegetables or a fresh salad.

Nutrition Count per Serving:

Approximately: 350 calories, 22g fat, 2g carbs, 34g protein, 1g fiber, 0g sugar

Lemon and Caper Chicken Piccata

Ingredients:

- 4 boneless, skinless chicken breasts
- 1/4 cup all-purpose flour
- 2 tablespoons olive oil
- 1/4 cup chicken broth
- 1/4 cup fresh lemon juice
- 2 tablespoons capers, rinsed
- 2 tablespoons fresh parsley, chopped
- Salt and pepper to taste

Instructions:

1. Pound the chicken breasts to an even thickness.
2. Season the flour with salt and pepper, then dredge the chicken breasts in the flour.
3. Heat olive oil in a large skillet over medium-high heat.
4. Cook the chicken breasts until golden brown and cooked through, about 4-5 minutes per side. Remove from the skillet and set aside.
5. In the same skillet, add the chicken broth, lemon juice, and capers. Bring to a boil and cook for 2 minutes.
6. Return the chicken to the skillet and simmer for an additional 2 minutes, coating the chicken with the sauce.
7. Sprinkle with fresh parsley.

How to Serve:

Serve immediately, optionally over a bed of pasta or with a side of roasted vegetables.

Nutrition Count per Serving:

Approximately: 280 calories, 12g fat, 8g carbs, 34g protein, 1g fiber, 1g sugar

Stuffed Peppers with Quinoa

Ingredients:

- 4 large bell peppers, tops cut off and seeds removed
- 1 cup cooked quinoa
- 1 cup black beans, drained and rinsed
- 1 cup corn kernels
- 1/2 cup diced tomatoes
- 1/4 cup red onion, finely chopped
- 1 teaspoon ground cumin
- 1 teaspoon chili powder
- 1/2 cup shredded cheddar cheese
- Salt and pepper to taste
- 1 tablespoon olive oil

Instructions:

1. Preheat the oven to 375°F (190°C).
2. In a large bowl, combine the cooked quinoa, black beans, corn, diced tomatoes, red onion, cumin, chili powder, salt, and pepper.
3. Stuff each bell pepper with the quinoa mixture and place in a baking dish.
4. Drizzle olive oil over the stuffed peppers.
5. Cover with foil and bake for 25 minutes.
6. Remove the foil, sprinkle the stuffed peppers with shredded cheddar cheese, and bake for an additional 10 minutes, or until the cheese is melted and bubbly.

How to Serve:

Serve warm, optionally with a dollop of sour cream or a side of salsa.

Nutrition Count per Serving:

Approximately: 300 calories, 10g fat, 40g carbs, 12g protein, 8g fiber, 6g sugar

Mediterranean Meatballs

Ingredients:

- 1 pound ground beef or lamb
- 1/2 cup breadcrumbs
- 1/4 cup grated Parmesan cheese
- 1/4 cup fresh parsley, chopped
- 1/4 cup onion, finely chopped
- 2 cloves garlic, minced
- 1 egg, beaten
- 1 teaspoon dried oregano
- 1 teaspoon dried mint
- Salt and pepper to taste
- 2 tablespoons olive oil
- 1 can (14 oz) crushed tomatoes
- 1/4 cup Kalamata olives, pitted and sliced
- 1/4 cup crumbled feta cheese

Instructions:

1. In a large bowl, combine the ground beef or lamb, breadcrumbs, Parmesan cheese, parsley, onion, garlic, beaten egg, oregano, mint, salt, and pepper. Mix until well combined.
2. Form the mixture into small meatballs.
3. Heat olive oil in a large skillet over medium heat. Add the meatballs and cook until browned on all sides, about 8-10 minutes.
4. Add the crushed tomatoes and Kalamata olives to the skillet. Bring to a simmer and cook for 15-20 minutes, or until the meatballs are cooked through.
5. Sprinkle with crumbled feta cheese before serving.

How to Serve:

Serve warm with a side of couscous or over a bed of rice.

Nutrition Count per Serving:

Approximately: 350 calories, 22g fat, 12g carbs, 26g protein, 2g fiber, 5g sugar

Rosemary Roasted Lamb

Ingredients:

- 1 boneless leg of lamb (about 4 pounds)

- 4 cloves garlic, minced

- 2 tablespoons fresh rosemary, chopped

- 2 tablespoons olive oil

- 1 tablespoon lemon juice

- Salt and pepper to taste

- 1/2 cup chicken broth

Instructions:

1. Preheat the oven to 375°F (190°C).

2. In a small bowl, mix together the minced garlic, chopped rosemary, olive oil, lemon juice, salt, and pepper.

3. Rub the mixture all over the lamb.

4. Place the lamb in a roasting pan and pour the chicken broth into the bottom of the pan.

5. Roast the lamb for 1.5 to 2 hours, or until the internal temperature reaches 145°F (63°C) for medium-rare.

6. Let the lamb rest for 10-15 minutes before slicing.

How to Serve:

Serve warm, sliced thinly, with roasted vegetables or potatoes.

Nutrition Count per Serving:

Approximately: 400 calories, 25g fat, 2g carbs, 40g protein, 1g fiber, 0g sugar

Greek Chicken Souvlaki

Ingredients:

- 2 pounds boneless, skinless chicken breasts, cut into 1-inch cubes

- 1/4 cup olive oil

- 3 tablespoons lemon juice

- 2 cloves garlic, minced

- 2 teaspoons dried oregano

- 1 teaspoon dried thyme

- Salt and pepper to taste

- Wooden skewers, soaked in water for 30 minutes

Instructions:

1. In a large bowl, combine the olive oil, lemon juice, minced garlic, oregano, thyme, salt, and pepper.

2. Add the chicken cubes and toss to coat. Marinate in the refrigerator for at least 30 minutes, or up to 2 hours.

3. Preheat the grill to medium-high heat.

4. Thread the marinated chicken onto the skewers.

5. Grill the chicken skewers for 10-12 minutes, turning occasionally, until the chicken is cooked through and lightly charred.

How to Serve:

Serve immediately with a side of tzatziki sauce, pita bread, and a Greek salad.

Nutrition Count per Serving:

Approximately: 300 calories, 14g fat, 2g carbs, 40g protein, 1g fiber, 1g sugar

Mediterranean Baked Cod

Ingredients:

- 4 cod fillets
- 2 tablespoons olive oil
- 1 lemon, sliced
- 1 cup cherry tomatoes, halved
- 1/4 cup Kalamata olives, pitted and halved
- 2 cloves garlic, minced
- 1 tablespoon fresh parsley, chopped
- 1 teaspoon dried oregano
- Salt and pepper to taste

Instructions:

1. Preheat the oven to 375°F (190°C).

2. Place the cod fillets in a baking dish and drizzle with olive oil.

3. Season with salt, pepper, and dried oregano.

4. Top with lemon slices, cherry tomatoes, Kalamata olives, and minced garlic.

5. Bake for 20-25 minutes, or until the cod is cooked through and flakes easily with a fork.

6. Garnish with fresh parsley before serving.

How to Serve:

Serve warm with a side of quinoa or a fresh green salad.

Nutrition Count per Serving:

Approximately: 250 calories, 10g fat, 6g carbs, 35g protein, 2g fiber, 2g sugar

Octopus Salad

Ingredients:

- 1 pound cooked octopus, cut into bite-sized pieces
- 1/4 cup red onion, thinly sliced
- 1/4 cup fresh parsley, chopped
- 1/4 cup Kalamata olives, pitted and sliced
- 1/4 cup cherry tomatoes, halved
- 2 tablespoons olive oil
- 1 tablespoon red wine vinegar
- 1 lemon, juiced
- Salt and pepper to taste

Instructions:

1. In a large bowl, combine the cooked octopus, red onion, parsley, Kalamata olives, and cherry tomatoes.
2. In a small bowl, whisk together the olive oil, red wine vinegar, lemon juice, salt, and pepper.
3. Pour the dressing over the octopus mixture and toss to combine.
4. Let the salad marinate in the refrigerator for at least 30 minutes before serving.

How to Serve:

Serve chilled or at room temperature as an appetizer or light dinner.

Nutrition Count per Serving:

Approximately: 200 calories, 10g fat, 6g carbs, 20g protein, 2g fiber, 2g sugar

Seafood Paella

Ingredients:

- 1 cup Arborio rice

- 2 tablespoons olive oil

- 1 onion, finely chopped

- 2 cloves garlic, minced

- 1 red bell pepper, diced

- 1/2 cup green peas

- 1/2 cup diced tomatoes

- 1/4 cup white wine

- 2 cups seafood broth

- 1/2 pound shrimp, peeled and deveined

- 1/2 pound mussels, cleaned and debearded

- 1/2 pound calamari, sliced into rings

- 1/4 cup fresh parsley, chopped

- 1 teaspoon smoked paprika

- Salt and pepper to taste

- Lemon wedges for serving

Instructions:

1. Heat the olive oil in a large skillet or paella pan over medium heat.

2. Add the chopped onion and garlic and sauté until softened, about 5 minutes.

3. Stir in the diced red bell pepper, green peas, and diced tomatoes. Cook for another 5 minutes.

4. Add the Arborio rice and smoked paprika, stirring to coat the rice with the vegetables and oil.

5. Pour in the white wine and cook until mostly evaporated, about 2 minutes.

6. Add the seafood broth, bring to a simmer, and cook for 15-20 minutes, stirring occasionally, until the rice is almost tender.

7. Arrange the shrimp, mussels, and calamari on top of the rice. Cover and cook for another 10 minutes, or until the seafood is cooked through and the mussels have opened.

8. Sprinkle with fresh parsley and season with salt and pepper.

How to Serve:

Serve hot with lemon wedges on the side.

Nutrition Count per Serving:

Approximately: 400 calories, 12g fat, 45g carbs, 28g protein, 4g fiber, 4g sugar

Chickpea and Spinach Stew

Ingredients:

- 1 can chickpeas, drained and rinsed
- 4 cups fresh spinach
- 1 onion, finely chopped
- 2 cloves garlic, minced
- 1 can diced tomatoes (14 oz)
- 2 cups vegetable broth
- 1 tablespoon olive oil
- 1 teaspoon ground cumin
- 1 teaspoon ground coriander
- 1/2 teaspoon smoked paprika
- Salt and pepper to taste

Instructions:

1. Heat olive oil in a large pot over medium heat.
2. Add the chopped onion and garlic, and sauté until softened, about 5 minutes.
3. Stir in the ground cumin, ground coriander, and smoked paprika, cooking for another 1-2 minutes until fragrant.
4. Add the diced tomatoes and vegetable broth, bringing the mixture to a simmer.
5. Stir in the chickpeas and fresh spinach. Cook for 10-15 minutes, or until the spinach is wilted and the stew is heated through.
6. Season with salt and pepper to taste.

How to Serve:

Serve hot with crusty bread or over a bed of rice.

Nutrition Count per Serving:

Approximately: 220 calories, 7g fat, 30g carbs, 10g protein, 8g fiber, 6g sugar

Grilled Eggplant with Herbs

Ingredients:

- 2 large eggplants, sliced into 1/2-inch rounds

- 3 tablespoons olive oil

- 2 cloves garlic, minced

- 1 tablespoon fresh basil, chopped

- 1 tablespoon fresh parsley, chopped

- Salt and pepper to taste

- Lemon wedges for serving

Instructions:

1. Preheat the grill to medium-high heat.

2. In a small bowl, mix together the olive oil, minced garlic, fresh basil, fresh parsley, salt, and pepper.

3. Brush the eggplant slices with the olive oil mixture.

4. Grill the eggplant slices for 4-5 minutes per side, or until tender and lightly charred.

5. Remove from the grill and sprinkle with additional herbs if desired.

How to Serve:

Serve warm with lemon wedges on the side.

Nutrition Count per Serving:

Approximately: 150 calories, 10g fat, 15g carbs, 2g protein, 6g fiber, 6g sugar

Roasted Zucchini with Garlic

Ingredients:

- 4 medium zucchinis, sliced into rounds

- 3 tablespoons olive oil

- 3 cloves garlic, minced

- 1 teaspoon dried thyme

- 1 teaspoon dried oregano

- Salt and pepper to taste

Instructions:

1. Preheat the oven to 400°F (200°C).

2. In a large bowl, toss the zucchini slices with olive oil, minced garlic, dried thyme, dried oregano, salt, and pepper.

3. Spread the zucchini slices in a single layer on a baking sheet.

4. Roast for 20-25 minutes, or until the zucchini is tender and lightly browned.

How to Serve:

Serve warm as a side dish or appetizer.

Nutrition Count per Serving:

Approximately: 120 calories, 8g fat, 10g carbs, 2g protein, 2g fiber, 4g sugar

Sautéed Spinach with Pine Nuts

Ingredients:

- 4 cups fresh spinach leaves

- 2 tablespoons olive oil

- 2 cloves garlic, minced

- 1/4 cup pine nuts

- Salt and pepper to taste

- 1 tablespoon lemon juice

Instructions:

1. Heat olive oil in a large skillet over medium heat.

2. Add the minced garlic and pine nuts, and sauté until the pine nuts are golden brown and the garlic is fragrant, about 2-3 minutes.

3. Add the spinach to the skillet and cook, stirring frequently, until wilted, about 3-4 minutes.

4. Season with salt, pepper, and lemon juice.

How to Serve:

Serve immediately as a side dish.

Nutrition Count per Serving:

Approximately: 150 calories, 12g fat, 6g carbs, 3g protein, 3g fiber, 1g sugar

Baked Stuffed Tomatoes

Ingredients:

- 6 large tomatoes

- 1 cup cooked quinoa

- 1/2 cup feta cheese, crumbled

- 1/4 cup red onion, finely chopped

- 2 cloves garlic, minced

- 2 tablespoons fresh basil, chopped

- 2 tablespoons olive oil

- Salt and pepper to taste

Instructions:

1. Preheat the oven to 375°F (190°C).

2. Slice the tops off the tomatoes and scoop out the insides. Reserve the tops.

3. In a bowl, combine the cooked quinoa, feta cheese, red onion, minced garlic, fresh basil, olive oil, salt, and pepper.

4. Stuff each tomato with the quinoa mixture and place the tops back on.

5. Arrange the stuffed tomatoes in a baking dish and bake for 25-30 minutes, or until the tomatoes are tender and the stuffing is heated through.

How to Serve:

Serve warm as a main course or side dish.

Nutrition Count per Serving:

Approximately: 200 calories, 10g fat, 20g carbs, 5g protein, 4g fiber, 5g sugar

Ratatouille

Ingredients:

- 1 eggplant, diced
- 1 zucchini, diced
- 1 red bell pepper, diced
- 1 yellow bell pepper, diced
- 1 onion, diced
- 4 cloves garlic, minced
- 2 cups diced tomatoes (canned or fresh)
- 1/4 cup olive oil
- 1 teaspoon dried thyme
- 1 teaspoon dried oregano
- Salt and pepper to taste
- 1/4 cup fresh basil, chopped

Instructions:

1. Preheat the oven to 375°F (190°C).
2. In a large bowl, combine the diced eggplant, zucchini, red bell pepper, yellow bell pepper, onion, minced garlic, diced tomatoes, olive oil, dried thyme, dried oregano, salt, and pepper.
3. Transfer the mixture to a large baking dish and spread it out evenly.
4. Bake for 45-50 minutes, or until the vegetables are tender and the flavors are well combined.
5. Stir in the fresh basil before serving.

How to Serve:

Serve warm as a main dish or side dish, optionally with crusty bread.

Nutrition Count per Serving:

Approximately: 180 calories, 12g fat, 18g carbs, 3g protein, 5g fiber, 8g sugar

CHAPTER 8

Mediterranean Sides and Treats

Quinoa Tabbouleh

Ingredients:

- 1 cup quinoa, rinsed

- 2 cups water

- 1 cup parsley, finely chopped

- 1/2 cup mint leaves, finely chopped

- 1/2 cup green onions, finely chopped

- 1 cup cherry tomatoes, diced

- 1 cucumber, diced

- 1/4 cup olive oil

- 1/4 cup lemon juice

- Salt and pepper to taste

Instructions:

1. In a medium saucepan, bring the water to a boil. Add the quinoa, reduce heat to low, cover, and simmer for 15 minutes, or until the quinoa is tender and the water is absorbed. Fluff with a fork and let cool.

2. In a large bowl, combine the cooked quinoa, parsley, mint, green onions, cherry tomatoes, and cucumber.

3. In a small bowl, whisk together the olive oil, lemon juice, salt, and pepper.

4. Pour the dressing over the quinoa mixture and toss to combine.

How to Serve:

Serve chilled or at room temperature as a refreshing side dish.

Nutrition Count per Serving:

Approximately: 200 calories, 10g fat, 25g carbs, 5g protein, 4g fiber, 2g sugar

Panzanella (Italian Bread Salad)

Ingredients:

- 4 cups day-old bread, cubed

- 2 cups cherry tomatoes, halved

- 1 cucumber, diced

- 1 red bell pepper, diced

- 1/2 red onion, thinly sliced

- 1/4 cup fresh basil, chopped

- 1/4 cup olive oil

- 2 tablespoons red wine vinegar

- Salt and pepper to taste

Instructions:

1. Preheat the oven to 375°F (190°C). Spread the bread cubes on a baking sheet and toast in the oven for 10-15 minutes, or until golden and crispy.

2. In a large bowl, combine the toasted bread cubes, cherry tomatoes, cucumber, red bell pepper, red onion, and fresh basil.

3. In a small bowl, whisk together the olive oil, red wine vinegar, salt, and pepper.

4. Pour the dressing over the salad and toss to combine. Let sit for at least 30 minutes before serving to allow the flavors to meld.

How to Serve:

Serve at room temperature as a hearty side dish.

Nutrition Count per Serving:

Approximately: 250 calories, 12g fat, 30g carbs, 5g protein, 3g fiber, 6g sugar

Greek Salad with Feta and Olives

Ingredients:

- 4 cups mixed greens

- 1 cup cherry tomatoes, halved

- 1 cucumber, sliced

- 1/2 red onion, thinly sliced

- 1/2 cup Kalamata olives, pitted and halved

- 1/2 cup feta cheese, crumbled

- 1/4 cup olive oil

- 2 tablespoons red wine vinegar

- 1 teaspoon dried oregano

- Salt and pepper to taste

Instructions:

1. In a large bowl, combine the mixed greens, cherry tomatoes, cucumber, red onion, Kalamata olives, and feta cheese.

2. In a small bowl, whisk together the olive oil, red wine vinegar, dried oregano, salt, and pepper.

3. Pour the dressing over the salad and toss to combine.

How to Serve:

Serve immediately as a fresh and tangy side dish.

Nutrition Count per Serving:

Approximately: 200 calories, 16g fat, 8g carbs, 5g protein, 2g fiber, 4g sugar

Mediterranean Chickpea Salad

Ingredients:

- 1 can chickpeas, drained and rinsed

- 1 cup cherry tomatoes, halved

- 1 cucumber, diced

- 1/4 red onion, finely chopped

- 1/4 cup fresh parsley, chopped

- 1/4 cup fresh mint, chopped

- 1/4 cup feta cheese, crumbled

- 1/4 cup olive oil

- 2 tablespoons lemon juice

- Salt and pepper to taste

Instructions:

1. In a large bowl, combine the chickpeas, cherry tomatoes, cucumber, red onion, parsley, mint, and feta cheese.

2. In a small bowl, whisk together the olive oil, lemon juice, salt, and pepper.

3. Pour the dressing over the salad and toss to combine.

How to Serve:

Serve chilled or at room temperature as a vibrant and nutritious side dish.

Nutrition Count per Serving:

Approximately: 250 calories, 14g fat, 24g carbs, 7g protein, 6g fiber, 5g sugar

Roasted Vegetable Salad

Ingredients:

- 1 red bell pepper, diced

- 1 yellow bell pepper, diced

- 1 zucchini, diced

- 1 eggplant, diced

- 1 red onion, diced

- 1/4 cup olive oil

- 2 tablespoons balsamic vinegar

- 1 teaspoon dried thyme

- 1 teaspoon dried oregano

- Salt and pepper to taste

- 2 cups mixed greens

Instructions:

1. Preheat the oven to 400°F (200°C).

2. In a large bowl, toss the diced bell peppers, zucchini, eggplant, and red onion with olive oil, balsamic vinegar, dried thyme, dried oregano, salt, and pepper.

3. Spread the vegetables in a single layer on a baking sheet and roast for 20-25 minutes, or until tender and slightly caramelized.

4. Let the vegetables cool slightly, then toss with mixed greens.

How to Serve:

Serve warm or at room temperature as a hearty and flavorful side dish.

Nutrition Count per Serving:

Approximately: 220 calories, 14g fat, 22g carbs, 3g protein, 5g fiber, 8g sugar

Lentil Soup with Vegetables

Ingredients:

- 1 cup lentils, rinsed
- 1 onion, finely chopped
- 2 carrots, diced
- 2 celery stalks, diced
- 2 cloves garlic, minced
- 1 can diced tomatoes (14 oz)
- 4 cups vegetable broth
- 1 teaspoon ground cumin
- 1 teaspoon ground coriander
- 1 bay leaf
- 2 tablespoons olive oil
- Salt and pepper to taste
- 1/4 cup fresh parsley, chopped

Instructions:

1. Heat the olive oil in a large pot over medium heat.
2. Add the chopped onion, carrots, and celery. Sauté until the vegetables are softened, about 5 minutes.
3. Stir in the minced garlic, ground cumin, and ground coriander. Cook for another 1-2 minutes until fragrant.
4. Add the lentils, diced tomatoes, vegetable broth, and bay leaf. Bring to a boil.
5. Reduce heat to low, cover, and simmer for 30-35 minutes, or until the lentils are tender.
6. Remove the bay leaf and season with salt and pepper.
7. Stir in the fresh parsley before serving.

How to Serve:

Serve hot with crusty bread or a side salad.

Nutrition Count per Serving:

Approximately: 250 calories, 8g fat, 36g carbs, 12g protein, 10g fiber, 6g sugar

Chicken Orzo Soup

Ingredients:

- 1 pound boneless, skinless chicken breasts
- 1 onion, finely chopped
- 2 carrots, diced
- 2 celery stalks, diced
- 2 cloves garlic, minced
- 1 cup orzo pasta
- 6 cups chicken broth
- 1 teaspoon dried thyme
- 1 teaspoon dried oregano
- 2 tablespoons olive oil
- Salt and pepper to taste
- 1/4 cup fresh parsley, chopped
- Juice of 1 lemon

Instructions:

1. Heat the olive oil in a large pot over medium heat.
2. Add the chopped onion, carrots, and celery. Sauté until the vegetables are softened, about 5 minutes.
3. Stir in the minced garlic, dried thyme, and dried oregano. Cook for another 1-2 minutes until fragrant.
4. Add the chicken breasts and chicken broth. Bring to a boil.
5. Reduce heat to low, cover, and simmer for 20-25 minutes, or until the chicken is cooked through.
6. Remove the chicken from the pot and shred it with two forks.
7. Return the shredded chicken to the pot and stir in the orzo pasta. Cook for an additional 10 minutes, or until the orzo is tender.
8. Season with salt, pepper, and lemon juice.
9. Stir in the fresh parsley before serving.

How to Serve:

Serve hot with a slice of lemon on the side.

Nutrition Count per Serving:

Approximately: 300 calories, 8g fat, 35g carbs, 22g protein, 3g fiber, 4g sugar

Moroccan Lamb Tagine

Ingredients:

- 1 pound lamb shoulder, cut into chunks

- 1 onion, finely chopped

- 2 carrots, diced

- 2 cloves garlic, minced

- 1 can chickpeas, drained and rinsed

- 1 cup diced tomatoes

- 1/2 cup dried apricots, chopped

- 2 cups beef broth

- 1 teaspoon ground cumin

- 1 teaspoon ground cinnamon

- 1 teaspoon ground turmeric

- 1/2 teaspoon ground ginger

- 2 tablespoons olive oil

- Salt and pepper to taste

- 1/4 cup fresh cilantro, chopped

Instructions:

1. Heat the olive oil in a large pot or tagine over medium heat.

2. Add the lamb chunks and brown on all sides. Remove the lamb and set aside.

3. In the same pot, add the chopped onion and carrots. Sauté until the vegetables are softened, about 5 minutes.

4. Stir in the minced garlic, ground cumin, ground cinnamon, ground turmeric, and ground ginger. Cook for another 1-2 minutes until fragrant.

5. Return the lamb to the pot and add the chickpeas, diced tomatoes, dried apricots, and beef broth. Bring to a boil.

6. Reduce heat to low, cover, and simmer for 1.5 to 2 hours, or until the lamb is tender.

7. Season with salt and pepper.

8. Stir in the fresh cilantro before serving.

How to Serve:

Serve hot over couscous or with crusty bread.

Nutrition Count per Serving:

Approximately: 400 calories, 18g fat, 40g carbs, 24g protein, 8g fiber, 12g sugar

Italian Vegetable Stew

Ingredients:

- 1 zucchini, diced
- 1 eggplant, diced
- 1 red bell pepper, diced
- 1 yellow bell pepper, diced
- 1 onion, chopped
- 2 cloves garlic, minced
- 1 can diced tomatoes (14 oz)
- 4 cups vegetable broth
- 1 teaspoon dried basil
- 1 teaspoon dried oregano
- 1 teaspoon dried thyme
- 2 tablespoons olive oil
- Salt and pepper to taste
- 1/4 cup fresh basil, chopped

Instructions:

1. Heat the olive oil in a large pot over medium heat.
2. Add the chopped onion and garlic. Sauté until the onion is softened, about 5 minutes.
3. Add the diced zucchini, eggplant, red bell pepper, and yellow bell pepper. Cook for 10 minutes, stirring occasionally.
4. Stir in the diced tomatoes, vegetable broth, dried basil, dried oregano, and dried thyme. Bring to a boil.
5. Reduce heat to low, cover, and simmer for 30 minutes, or until the vegetables are tender.
6. Season with salt and pepper.
7. Stir in the fresh basil before serving.

How to Serve:

Serve hot with a drizzle of olive oil and crusty bread on the side.

Nutrition Count per Serving:

Approximately: 180 calories, 8g fat, 24g carbs, 4g protein, 6g fiber, 8g sugar

Greek Lemon Chicken Soup

Ingredients:

- 1 pound boneless, skinless chicken breasts
- 6 cups chicken broth
- 1/2 cup orzo pasta
- 2 eggs
- 1/4 cup lemon juice
- 1 onion, finely chopped
- 2 carrots, diced
- 2 celery stalks, diced
- 2 cloves garlic, minced
- 2 tablespoons olive oil
- Salt and pepper to taste
- 1/4 cup fresh dill, chopped

Instructions:

1. Heat the olive oil in a large pot over medium heat.
2. Add the chopped onion, carrots, and celery. Sauté until the vegetables are softened, about 5 minutes.
3. Stir in the minced garlic and cook for another 1-2 minutes.
4. Add the chicken breasts and chicken broth. Bring to a boil.
5. Reduce heat to low, cover, and simmer for 20-25 minutes, or until the chicken is cooked through.
6. Remove the chicken from the pot and shred it with two forks. Return the shredded chicken to the pot.
7. Stir in the orzo pasta and cook for an additional 10 minutes, or until the orzo is tender.
8. In a small bowl, whisk the eggs and lemon juice together. Slowly add a ladleful of hot soup to the egg mixture, whisking constantly to temper the eggs.
9. Slowly pour the egg mixture back into the soup, stirring constantly.
10. Season with salt, pepper, and fresh dill.

How to Serve:

Serve hot with a slice of lemon on the side.

Nutrition Count per Serving:

Approximately: 300 calories, 8g fat, 30g carbs, 24g protein, 3g fiber, 4g sugar

Tzatziki Sauce

Ingredients:

- 1 cup Greek yogurt

- 1 cucumber, grated and excess water squeezed out

- 2 cloves garlic, minced

- 1 tablespoon fresh dill, chopped

- 1 tablespoon fresh mint, chopped

- 1 tablespoon olive oil

- 1 tablespoon lemon juice

- Salt and pepper to taste

Instructions:

1. In a medium bowl, combine the Greek yogurt, grated cucumber, minced garlic, dill, mint, olive oil, lemon juice, salt, and pepper.

2. Mix well until all ingredients are evenly distributed.

How to Serve:

Serve chilled as a dip with pita bread or fresh vegetables, or as a sauce for grilled meats.

Nutrition Count per Serving:

Approximately: 80 calories, 4g fat, 6g carbs, 6g protein, 0g fiber, 3g sugar

Hummus

Ingredients:

- 1 can chickpeas, drained and rinsed

- 1/4 cup tahini

- 2 tablespoons olive oil

- 2 cloves garlic, minced

- 1 lemon, juiced

- 1/2 teaspoon ground cumin

- Salt and pepper to taste

- 1/4 cup water (as needed for consistency)

Instructions:

1. In a food processor, combine the chickpeas, tahini, olive oil, minced garlic, lemon juice, ground cumin, salt, and pepper.

2. Blend until smooth, adding water as needed to reach desired consistency.

How to Serve:

Serve as a dip with pita bread or fresh vegetables, or as a spread for sandwiches.

Nutrition Count per Serving:

Approximately: 140 calories, 8g fat, 14g carbs, 4g protein, 4g fiber, 1g sugar

Pesto Sauce

Ingredients:

- 2 cups fresh basil leaves

- 1/2 cup Parmesan cheese, grated

- 1/2 cup pine nuts

- 2 cloves garlic, minced

- 1/2 cup olive oil

- Salt and pepper to taste

Instructions:

1. In a food processor, combine the basil leaves, Parmesan cheese, pine nuts, and minced garlic.

2. Blend until the ingredients are finely chopped.

3. With the food processor running, slowly drizzle in the olive oil until the mixture is smooth.

4. Season with salt and pepper to taste.

How to Serve:

Serve as a sauce for pasta, a spread for sandwiches, or a dip for bread.

Nutrition Count per Serving:

Approximately: 180 calories, 18g fat, 2g carbs, 4g protein, 1g fiber, 0g sugar

Tapenade

Ingredients:

- 1 cup Kalamata olives, pitted

- 1/4 cup capers, rinsed and drained

- 2 cloves garlic, minced

- 2 tablespoons fresh parsley, chopped

- 2 tablespoons lemon juice

- 1/4 cup olive oil

- Salt and pepper to taste

Instructions:

1. In a food processor, combine the Kalamata olives, capers, minced garlic, parsley, and lemon juice.

2. Blend until finely chopped.

3. With the food processor running, slowly drizzle in the olive oil until the mixture is smooth.

4. Season with salt and pepper to taste.

How to Serve:

Serve as a dip with crackers or bread, or as a spread for sandwiches.

Nutrition Count per Serving:

Approximately: 100 calories, 10g fat, 1g carbs, 1g protein, 1g fiber, 0g sugar

Romesco Sauce

Ingredients:

- 2 roasted red bell peppers, peeled and seeded

- 1/2 cup almonds, toasted

- 2 cloves garlic, minced

- 1/4 cup olive oil

- 2 tablespoons red wine vinegar

- 1 teaspoon smoked paprika

- Salt and pepper to taste

Instructions:

1. In a food processor, combine the roasted red bell peppers, toasted almonds, minced garlic, olive oil, red wine vinegar, and smoked paprika.

2. Blend until smooth.

3. Season with salt and pepper to taste.

How to Serve:

Serve as a dip with vegetables or bread, or as a sauce for grilled meats or seafood.

Nutrition Count per Serving:

Approximately: 120 calories, 10g fat, 6g carbs, 2g protein, 2g fiber, 2g sugar

Greek Yogurt with Honey and Nuts

Ingredients:

- 2 cups Greek yogurt

- 4 tablespoons honey

- 1/4 cup walnuts, chopped

- 1/4 cup almonds, chopped

- 1/4 teaspoon ground cinnamon (optional)

Instructions:

1. Divide the Greek yogurt into four serving bowls.

2. Drizzle each serving with 1 tablespoon of honey.

3. Sprinkle the chopped walnuts and almonds evenly over the yogurt.

4. Optionally, sprinkle a pinch of ground cinnamon on top.

How to Serve:

Serve immediately as a simple and nutritious dessert.

Nutrition Count per Serving:

Approximately: 250 calories, 12g fat, 25g carbs, 12g protein, 2g fiber, 20g sugar

Baklava

Ingredients:

- 1 package phyllo dough, thawed
- 2 cups walnuts, finely chopped
- 1 cup almonds, finely chopped
- 1 teaspoon ground cinnamon
- 1 cup butter, melted
- 1 cup honey
- 1/2 cup water
- 1/2 cup sugar
- 1 teaspoon vanilla extract

Instructions:

1. Preheat the oven to 350°F (175°C).
2. In a bowl, combine the chopped walnuts, almonds, and ground cinnamon.
3. Brush a 9x13-inch baking dish with melted butter. Layer 10 sheets of phyllo dough in the dish, brushing each sheet with melted butter before adding the next.
4. Sprinkle a thin layer of the nut mixture over the phyllo.
5. Layer 5 more sheets of phyllo, brushing each with melted butter. Repeat the process until all the nut mixture is used, ending with 10 layers of phyllo on top.
6. Using a sharp knife, cut the baklava into diamond or square shapes.
7. Bake for 45-50 minutes, or until golden brown and crisp.
8. In a saucepan, combine the honey, water, sugar, and vanilla extract. Bring to a boil, then reduce heat and simmer for 10 minutes.
9. Pour the hot honey mixture over the baked baklava. Let it cool completely before serving.

How to Serve:

Serve at room temperature as a rich and indulgent dessert.

Nutrition Count per Serving:

Approximately: 350 calories, 22g fat, 38g carbs, 4g protein, 2g fiber, 25g sugar

Lemon Olive Oil Cake

Ingredients:

- 1 1/2 cups all-purpose flour
- 1/2 teaspoon baking powder
- 1/2 teaspoon baking soda
- 1/4 teaspoon salt
- 1 cup granulated sugar
- 3 large eggs
- 1/2 cup olive oil
- 1/2 cup plain Greek yogurt
- 1/4 cup lemon juice
- Zest of 1 lemon
- 1 teaspoon vanilla extract
- Powdered sugar for dusting (optional)

Instructions:

1. Preheat the oven to 350°F (175°C). Grease and flour a 9-inch round cake pan.
2. In a bowl, whisk together the flour, baking powder, baking soda, and salt.
3. In another bowl, beat the sugar and eggs until pale and thick. Gradually add the olive oil, yogurt, lemon juice, lemon zest, and vanilla extract, mixing until well combined.
4. Gradually add the dry ingredients to the wet ingredients, mixing until just combined.
5. Pour the batter into the prepared cake pan.
6. Bake for 30-35 minutes, or until a toothpick inserted into the center comes out clean.
7. Allow the cake to cool in the pan for 10 minutes, then transfer to a wire rack to cool completely.
8. Dust with powdered sugar before serving, if desired.

How to Serve:

Serve at room temperature with a cup of tea or coffee.

Nutrition Count per Serving:

Approximately: 280 calories, 14g fat, 34g carbs, 4g protein, 1g fiber, 18g sugar

Ricotta and Fig Tart

Ingredients:

- 1 pre-made tart crust

- 1 cup ricotta cheese

- 1/4 cup honey

- 1 teaspoon vanilla extract

- 1/2 teaspoon ground cinnamon

- 6-8 fresh figs, sliced

Instructions:

1. Preheat the oven to 350°F (175°C). Place the tart crust in a tart pan and bake according to package instructions. Let it cool.

2. In a bowl, combine the ricotta cheese, honey, vanilla extract, and ground cinnamon. Mix until smooth.

3. Spread the ricotta mixture evenly over the cooled tart crust.

4. Arrange the fig slices on top of the ricotta mixture.

How to Serve:

Serve immediately or chill in the refrigerator until ready to serve.

Nutrition Count per Serving:

Approximately: 250 calories, 12g fat, 30g carbs, 6g protein, 2g fiber, 20g sugar

Pistachio Ice Cream

Ingredients:

- 1 1/2 cups shelled pistachios
- 1 cup granulated sugar
- 2 cups whole milk
- 1 cup heavy cream
- 4 large egg yolks
- 1 teaspoon vanilla extract
- A pinch of salt

Instructions:

1. In a food processor, finely grind the pistachios with 1/2 cup of sugar until they form a paste.
2. In a medium saucepan, combine the milk, heavy cream, and remaining 1/2 cup of sugar. Heat over medium heat until the mixture is hot but not boiling.
3. In a bowl, whisk the egg yolks. Gradually add a ladleful of the hot milk mixture to the yolks, whisking constantly to temper the eggs.
4. Pour the egg mixture back into the saucepan and cook over medium heat, stirring constantly, until the mixture thickens enough to coat the back of a spoon.
5. Remove from heat and stir in the pistachio paste, vanilla extract, and a pinch of salt. Mix until well combined.
6. Strain the mixture through a fine mesh sieve into a bowl to remove any lumps.
7. Chill the mixture in the refrigerator for at least 4 hours or overnight.
8. Churn the mixture in an ice cream maker according to the manufacturer's instructions.
9. Transfer the ice cream to a container and freeze for at least 2 hours before serving.

How to Serve:

Serve scoops of pistachio ice cream in bowls or cones.

Nutrition Count per Serving:

Approximately: 300 calories, 20g fat, 28g carbs, 6g protein, 2g fiber, 22g sugar

CHAPTER 9

Incorporating the Mediterranean Diet in Daily Life

Incorporating the Mediterranean Diet into your daily life means embracing a way of eating and living that focuses on balance, enjoyment, and sustainability. Here's how to seamlessly integrate the principles of this diet into your routine:

Embrace Fresh, Whole Foods

- **Choose Seasonal Produce:** Make it a habit to buy fresh, seasonal fruits and vegetables. Seasonal produce not only tastes better but also retains more nutrients.

- **Cook from Scratch:** Make your own meals as often as you can with whole, unadulterated products. This allows you to control what goes into your food and avoid additives and preservatives.

- **Make Cooking a Joyful Experience**

- **Simplify Recipes:** Start with simple Mediterranean recipes that require minimal ingredients and effort. Gradually experiment with more complex dishes as you become comfortable.

- **Involve Family and Friends:** Cooking is a social activity. To make it more enjoyable and less of a chore, involve family members or friends in meal preparation.

Develop a Routine

- **Plan Your Meals:** Spend some time each week planning your meals. This helps you stick to the diet and ensures you have all the ingredients you need.

- **Prep in Batches:** Prepare ingredients or meals in batches to save time during the week. For example, cook a large batch of grains or chop vegetables in advance.

Focus on Flavor

- **Use Herbs and Spices:** When at all feasible, cook your meals.Use a range of herbs and spices to give your food flavor without using too much salt or bad fat.made from start with whole, raw components.

- **Explore New Ingredients:** Try new Mediterranean ingredients, such as different types of olives, cheeses, and grains, to keep your meals interesting.

Stay Hydrated

- **Drink Plenty of Water:** Water is the main beverage of the Mediterranean Diet. Try to have eight glasses of water or more each day.

- **Moderate Wine Consumption:** If you drink alcohol, consider enjoying a glass of red wine with your meals, as is traditional in Mediterranean cultures.

Balance and Moderation

- **Portion Control:** Pay attention to portion sizes. The Mediterranean Diet emphasizes balance, so enjoy a variety of foods in moderation.

- **Occasional Treats:** Allow yourself to indulge in sweets or red meat occasionally, without guilt. The key is moderation, not restriction.

Enjoy the Process

- **Mindful Preparation:** Enjoy the process of cooking and preparing your meals. View it as a time to relax and be creative.

- **Savor Your Meals:** Take the time to savor your food and appreciate the flavors. Eating slowly and mindfully can enhance your dining experience.

Focus on these practical strategies and seamlessly integrate the Mediterranean Diet into your daily life. This approach enhances your physical health and promotes a more enjoyable and sustainable way of life.

Physical Activity and Exercise

A key component of the Mediterranean diet is regular physical activity, which greatly enhances general health and wellbeing. It's not necessary to make incorporating exercise into your everyday routine difficult or time-consuming. Here's how you can make physical activity a natural and enjoyable part of your life:

Daily Movement

Moving around every day is part of the Mediterranean lifestyle. Set a daily goal to spend at least 30 minutes doing moderate physical activity. This can be as easy as going for a brisk walk, which is great for your heart and gives you a chance to enjoy the fresh air and decompress.

Enjoyable Activities

Choose activities that you genuinely enjoy, as you are more likely to stick with them long-term. Whether it's swimming, dancing, cycling, or gardening, find what makes you happy and incorporate it into your routine. Engaging in enjoyable activities ensures that exercise feels less like a chore and more like a part of your lifestyle.

Incorporate Exercise into Daily Tasks

Look for methods to include exercise into your everyday responsibilities. For example, take the stairs instead of the elevator, walk or cycle for short errands instead of driving, or do household chores that require physical effort, such as cleaning or gardening. Over time, these modest adjustments may have a big positive impact on your health.

Social Exercise

Exercise can also be a social activity. Join a local sports club, attend group fitness classes, or simply go for a walk with friends or family. Social exercise keeps you physically active, strengthens social bonds, and provides emotional support.

Strength and Flexibility

In addition to cardiovascular activities, incorporate strength and flexibility exercises into your routine. Incorporating weights or resistance bands for strength training promotes the preservation of bone density and muscle mass. Exercises for flexibility, such as yoga or stretching, enhance joint health and help avoid accidents.

Consistency is Key

Consistency is the key to reaping the benefits of physical activity. Choose a regimen that works for your lifestyle and follow it. Even on busy days, try to find a few minutes for a quick walk or stretching exercises. Remember, any movement is better than none.

Listen to Your Body

While it's important to stay active, listening to your body is equally important. Avoid over-exertion and allow time for rest and recovery. If you feel pain or discomfort, modify your activities and seek medical advice if required.

You can reap a host of health advantages from incorporating regular physical activity into your daily routine, such as better weight control, longevity, higher mental well-being, and cardiovascular health improvements. A happier, more contented life might result from adopting this Mediterranean lifestyle component.

Mindful Eating Practices

Mindful eating is also a key component of the Mediterranean lifestyle, emphasizing the importance of enjoying food and being present during meals. By adopting mindful eating practices, you can enhance your relationship with food, improve digestion, and enjoy a more satisfying dining experience. Here are some tips to help you eat mindfully:

Slow Down and Savor Your Food

Eat mindfully and gently, savoring every meal. This allows you to fully appreciate your food's flavors, textures, and aromas. Eating slowly also gives your body time to signal when you are full, helping to prevent overeating.

Eliminate Distractions

Avoid distractions during meals, such as watching TV, using your phone, or working. Focus solely on the act of eating and the experience of enjoying your meal. This helps you become more aware of what and how much you eat.

Listen to Your Body

Observe your body's signals of hunger and fullness. Eat till you are satisfied, not too full, and quit when you are hungry again. By listening to your body, you can better regulate your food intake and avoid overeating.

Appreciate Your Food

Take a moment to appreciate the food on your plate. Consider where it came from, how it was prepared, and the effort that went into making it. This practice can enhance your gratitude for the meal and make the eating experience more enjoyable.

Engage Your Senses

Engage all your senses while eating. Notice the colors, smells, and presentation of your food. Enjoy the taste and texture with each bite. This sensory engagement can make meals more satisfying and enjoyable.

Practice Portion Control

Keeping an eye on portion sizes is part of mindful eating. Serve yourself reasonable portions and avoid eating directly from large packages or containers. This helps you control your intake and prevents overeating.

Chew Thoroughly

Chewing your food thoroughly aids digestion and allows you to enjoy the flavors fully. It also slows the eating process, giving your brain time to register that you are eating and helping you feel full sooner.

Create a Pleasant Eating Environment

Set up a pleasant and inviting eating environment. Use nice plates, set the table, and create a calm atmosphere. A positive environment can make meals more enjoyable and encourage mindful eating.

Reflect on Your Eating Habits

Take time to reflect on your eating habits and how they make you feel. Take note of which foods give you a boost of energy or a slump, and modify your diet accordingly. This reflection can help you make healthier choices that meet your body's needs.

Enjoy Social Meals

The Mediterranean lifestyle revolves around eating meals together with friends and family. Enjoying food in a social setting can enhance the dining experience, foster connections, and encourage mindful eating practices.

You may strengthen your overall well-being, improve your digestion, and create a healthy relationship with food by adopting these mindful eating techniques into your daily routine. Being present and fully appreciating your food is the essence of mindful eating; it has nothing to do with rigid guidelines or limitations.

Social and Cultural Aspects of the Diet

The Mediterranean Diet is deeply rooted in the social and cultural traditions of the Mediterranean region. It's not just about what you eat, but also about how you eat and the cultural practices surrounding food. Embracing these social and cultural aspects can enhance your overall well-being and bring more enjoyment to your meals.

Eating as a Social Activity

In Mediterranean cultures, meals are often shared with family and friends. Eating together is a time to connect, share stories, and enjoy each other's company. Eating with others has the potential to enhance emotional health, lower stress levels, and provide a feeling of community.

Benefits:

- **Enhanced Emotional Well-Being:** Eating meals together with those you love can make you feel happy and like you belong.

- **Reduced Stress:** Social interactions during meals can help you relax and unwind.

- **Stronger Community Bonds:** Regular shared meals strengthen relationships and community ties.

Enjoying Meals at a Leisurely Pace

Mediterranean cultures prioritize taking time to enjoy meals rather than rushing through them. This leisurely approach to eating allows you to savor your food, aids digestion, and promotes mindful eating.

Benefits:

- **Improved Digestion:** Eating slowly can help your body digest food more efficiently.

- **Mindful Eating:** Eating slowly allows you to savor the flavors and textures of your food, which increases your level of contentment.

Celebrating Food and Traditions

Food is an integral part of Mediterranean celebrations and traditions. From family gatherings to local festivals, food is central in bringing people together and celebrating life's moments. Embracing these traditions can add joy and meaning to your meals.

Benefits:

- **Cultural Enrichment:** Food traditions can deepen your understanding and appreciation of Mediterranean cultures.

- **Joyful Eating Experiences:** Celebratory meals and traditions add fun and excitement to your diet.

Incorporating Rituals

In Mediterranean cultures, certain rituals are associated with meals, such as blessing the food, expressing gratitude, or enjoying an aperitif before dinner. These rituals can enhance the dining experience and promote a sense of mindfulness and gratitude.

Benefits:

- **Mindfulness:** Rituals can help you focus on the present moment and appreciate your meal.

- **Gratitude:** Expressing thanks for your food can foster a positive relationship with what you eat.

Local and Seasonal Eating

The Mediterranean Diet emphasizes eating locally grown and seasonal foods. This not only guarantees the nutritious content and freshness of your meals, but it also helps sustainably and benefits nearby farmers.

Benefits:

- **Freshness and Flavor:** Seasonal foods are often fresher and more flavorful.

- **Nutritional Value:** Local and seasonal produce tends to have higher nutrient content.

- **Environmental Sustainability:** Promoting local agriculture reduces your carbon footprint and promotes sustainable farming practices.

Embracing Variety and Balance

Mediterranean meals are diverse and balanced, incorporating a wide range of food groups and flavors. This variety ensures that you get a broad spectrum of nutrients and keeps your meals interesting.

Benefits:

- **Nutritional Balance:** A varied diet ensures you receive all essential nutrients.

- **Culinary Enjoyment:** Trying different foods and recipes keeps your diet exciting and enjoyable.

To fully embrace the Mediterranean Diet, incorporate its social and cultural aspects into your daily life. Make an effort to share meals with family and friends, take time to enjoy your food, celebrate traditions, and appreciate the cultural richness of the Mediterranean way of eating. Doing so can enhance your overall well-being and enjoy a more fulfilling, balanced lifestyle.

CHAPTER 10

28-Day Meal Plan

Day	Breakfast	Lunch	Snack	Dinner
1	Greek Yogurt Breakfast Bowl	Greek Chicken Salad	Bread with Herb Curd	Baked Salmon with Herbs
2	Mediterranean Omelet	Mediterranean Tuna Salad	Bell Peppers Stuffed with Feta and Dill	Lemon and Caper Chicken Piccata
3	Bulgur Wheat Cereal with Apples and Almonds	Falafel Wraps	Avocado and Lime Guacamole	Stuffed Peppers with Quinoa
4	Ricotta and Fruit Bruschetta	Grilled Vegetable Panini	Roasted Chickpeas	Mediterranean Meatballs
5	Savory Feta, Spinach, and Red Pepper Muffins	Pita with Hummus and Veggies	Stuffed Grape Leaves	Rosemary Roasted Lamb
6	Oatmeal with Figs, Almonds, and Chia Seeds	Stuffed Portobello Mushrooms	Hummus with Veggies	Greek Chicken Souvlaki

7	Banana Almond Oatmeal Smoothie	Stuffed Zucchini Boats	Greek Yogurt Dip with Cucumber	Mediterranean Baked Cod
8	Apricot and Hazelnut Smoothie	Spinach and Feta Quesadilla	Zucchini Fritters	Octopus Salad
9	Green Detox Juice	Grilled Shrimp Skewers	Spinach and Feta Stuffed Mushrooms	Seafood Paella
10	Citrus Carrot Juice	Chickpea and Avocado Sandwich	Tomato Bruschetta	Chickpea and Spinach Stew
11	Tomato and Feta Frittata	Roasted Red Pepper and Hummus Wrap	Bread with Herb Curd	Grilled Eggplant with Herbs
12	Bell Pepper and Onion Scramble	Lentil and Quinoa Patties	Bell Peppers Stuffed with Feta and Dill	Roasted Zucchini with Garlic
13	Avocado Toast with Cherry Tomatoes	Chicken and Spinach Salad	Avocado and Lime Guacamole	Sautéed Spinach with Pine Nuts
14	Almond Butter and Banana Smoothie	Couscous and Roasted Vegetable Bowl	Roasted Chickpeas	Baked Stuffed Tomatoes
15	Blueberry and Walnut Oatmeal	Tuna and Roasted Vegetable Bowl	Stuffed Grape Leaves	Ratatouille

16	Greek Yogurt Breakfast Bowl	Greek Chicken Salad	Hummus with Veggies	Baked Salmon with Herbs
17	Mediterranean Omelet	Mediterranean Tuna Salad	Greek Yogurt Dip with Cucumber	Lemon and Caper Chicken Piccata
18	Bulgur Wheat Cereal with Apples and Almonds	Falafel Wraps	Zucchini Fritters	Stuffed Peppers with Quinoa
19	Ricotta and Fruit Bruschetta	Grilled Vegetable Panini	Spinach and Feta Stuffed Mushrooms	Mediterranean Meatballs
20	Savory Feta, Spinach, and Red Pepper Muffins	Pita with Hummus and Veggies	Tomato Bruschetta	Rosemary Roasted Lamb
21	Oatmeal with Figs, Almonds, and Chia Seeds	Stuffed Portobello Mushrooms	Bread with Herb Curd	Greek Chicken Souvlaki
22	Banana Almond Oatmeal Smoothie	Stuffed Zucchini Boats	Bell Peppers Stuffed with Feta and Dill	Mediterranean Baked Cod
23	Apricot and Hazelnut Smoothie	Spinach and Feta Quesadilla	Avocado and Lime Guacamole	Octopus Salad
24	Green Detox Juice	Grilled Shrimp Skewers	Roasted Chickpeas	Seafood Paella

25	Citrus Carrot Juice	Chickpea and Avocado Sandwich	Stuffed Grape Leaves	Chickpea and Spinach Stew
26	Tomato and Feta Frittata	Roasted Red Pepper and Hummus Wrap	Hummus with Veggies	Grilled Eggplant with Herbs
27	Bell Pepper and Onion Scramble	Lentil and Quinoa Patties	Greek Yogurt Dip with Cucumber	Roasted Zucchini with Garlic
28	Avocado Toast with Cherry Tomatoes	Chicken and Spinach Salad	Zucchini Fritters	Sautéed Spinach with Pine Nuts

Conclusion

As you reach the end of "Mediterranean Diet Cookbook for Beginners," I hope you have gained a deeper understanding and appreciation for the Mediterranean way of eating and living. The Mediterranean Diet is not just a set of dietary guidelines but a holistic lifestyle promoting overall well-being, longevity, and joy.

Throughout this book, you have discovered a variety of delicious and nutritious recipes that embody the core principles of the Mediterranean Diet. By emphasizing fresh, whole foods, healthy fats, lean proteins, and plenty of fruits and vegetables, you are nourishing your body with essential nutrients that ensure optimal health. The recipes provided are not only flavorful and satisfying but also designed to be easy to prepare, empowering you to incorporate this diet into your daily routine with ease.

In addition to the culinary aspects, the Mediterranean lifestyle encompasses regular physical activity, mindful eating practices, and the importance of social connections. By incorporating these elements into your life, you can achieve a balanced, fulfilling, and healthy existence.

As you continue your journey with the Mediterranean Diet, remember that it's about progress, not perfection. Small, consistent changes can lead to significant improvements in your health and quality of life. But more than that, it's about enjoying the process, experimenting with new recipes, and most importantly, savoring every bite. This approach will not only make your journey more enjoyable but also keep you motivated and positive.

Thank you for joining me on this journey to a healthier, happier you. May the recipes and tips in this book inspire you to embrace the Mediterranean way of life and experience all the benefits it has to offer.